QUEEN ANNE'S SCHOOL, CAVERSHAM
The First Hundred Years

Miss Holmes
1894-1917

Miss Scott
1977-1993

Miss Moore
1918-1938

Miss Challis
1958-1977

Miss Elliot
1939-1957

QUEEN ANNE'S SCHOOL, CAVERSHAM

The First Hundred Years

Edited by
Mary Driver and Audrey Scott

Phillimore

1994

Published by
PHILLIMORE & CO. LTD.,
Shopwyke Manor Barn, Chichester, West Sussex

ISBN 0 85033 892 1

Printed and bound in Great Britain by
THE BATH PRESS

Contents

List of Illustrations

Frontispiece: The five headmistresses

Acknowledgements

A history of any school requires a great deal of research and the co-operation of many people. The History Committee was formed to organise this book in commemoration of Queen Anne's School's first centenary.

It is with pleasure that we record our indebtedness to our authors:

Miss M. J. Challis

Mrs. H. McCall (née Sharpe)

Mrs. C. Obolensky (née Sharpe)

Mrs. J. Selby Green (née Hogarth)

Our thanks are due to the many Old Girls who have lent photographs and recounted anecdotes; our thanks to Mrs. A. Wheeldon at the Greycoat Foundation Archives, without whose help and knowledge this book would have been lacking in information and historic figures.

Last but not least go our thanks to Dr. H. Brand, the librarian and archivist at Queen Anne's School.

Foreword

This fascinating account of the first hundred years of Queen Anne's School gives a wonderful picture of the development of the present school from small beginnings, backed by faith and commitment to giving girls the best possible all-round education in a happy and Christian environment, with a continuing emphasis on service to others both within the School community and locally, nationally and internationally outside the School.

How fortunate Queen Anne's has been in its headmistresses. Each has made her highly individual contribution yet all have been committed to the same ideals. In turn they have moved with the times and adapted the school curriculum and the various school activities to the changing rôle of women without losing the sense of community in which staff and girls work together in harmony.

My first impression of Queen Anne's over 40 years ago was that it was a happy school. That happy atmosphere pervades this history and greets visitors to the school today; it continues to encourage parents to entrust their daughters to Queen Anne's, it attracts potential staff who come for interviews, and it makes the work of Governors a joy.

Long may Queen Anne's continue in 'Quietness and Strength', giving girls the means to develop their talents to the full and to play their part in the wider sphere in the years ahead.

Dr. D. Muriel Hall

Costume worn at the Grey Coat Hospital, 1701-1875.

The School

I lay my pen down in reflective mood,
And leave that other world of long ago,
When thought was simpler, right and wrong defined,
And life, untroubled, kept its even flow.

What did we learn in those young, heedless years?
Not the false values of this present day,
But your own standards: These you set
For guidance in our work, as at our play.

We took them with us into distant lands;
Through wars, through so-called peace, we found them sure:
And whether calm or chaos be our lot,
in 'Quietness and Strength' may we endure.

Alice Alment (née Slythe), 1894-1903

Chapter 1

How it all Began

Picture, if you will, eight merchants gathered together at the end of the 17th century in a house in Westminster. They are not wealthy, most of them are tradesmen of the time. There are Samuel Boulte, and Richard Ffyler, the draper; John Holmes, a seller of 'sope' and candles, with Robert Maddock, a 'cheesemonger'; Samuel Michell, a bookseller, and John Webbe; John Wilkins and Thomas Wisdome, a trader in brooms and leather goods, complete the group. One thing binds them together, and that is their determination to do whatever they can to help children in their city who are trapped in poverty and for whom the life of the streets seems the only possible future. To many men the task might have seemed so enormous that it would be entirely beyond their ability to do anything worthwhile; but those eight merchants were made of sterner stuff, and so from this tiny beginning was born a great Foundation which over the centuries has influenced the lives of thousands upon thousands.

From that first formal meeting on 30 November 1698, the plans for the future were enthusiastically unfolded, with everything done in a business-like way. Minutes were kept, and from the early meetings there were two Minute Books: one was apparently written by whoever acted as chairman each meeting, and though probably very accurate it was often nearly illegible and was referred to as the 'Ruff' or 'Fowl' book; the other was neatly copied out with reasonably correct spelling and this was the 'Fair Minute Book'. These men showed from the very beginning their care for detail and accuracy. The meeting was held in a house they had taken in Broad Sanctuary, in the parish of St Margaret's, Westminster, and it was here they intended to set up their school. Their purpose, as stated in the First Minutes, was to help 40 children: 'The greatest objects of charity they could find', who were to be 'educated in sober and vertuous Principles and instructed in the Christian religion'. At that time it was widely held to be the duty of a Christian to provide Christian teaching for poor children, so the eight merchants were in tune with some of their contemporaries. Where it seemed they perhaps improved on the record of others was in the great care they took over all the little details in the setting-up of their school, and the immense amount of time they continued to devote to its needs and interests. Their school was not to be somewhere which would benefit the children for only a short time but they were to be placed as apprentices 'to Honest masters, who should take care, as well of their good Principles as instruct them how to get an honest livelyhood by their labours and industry in the world'.

No charity school could exist on enthusiasm and principles alone, and these eight businessmen were ready to invest their own money to further their plans. They decided to meet each week, and at their second meeting each one subscribed five shillings to make their plans reality, with a further seven shillings and sixpence added for each one a week later. Robert Maddock's success with his cheeses seems to have qualified him for the position of Treasurer. The children were to be clothed 'for their Incouragement in their learning', and in this as in so much else the practical side of the Founders was shown, for, having acquired the linen needed to form the necessary 'bands', they promptly enlisted the help of their wives and daughters to make it up. School uniform has always brought its problems but for the early school these were different, for it proved necessary to restrict the wearing of full uniform, including a grey coat, to use on Sundays and other holy days when the children attended church. There were other problems too: when the boys were being prepared for their annual service a few years after the school opened, the grey caps were found to be very dirty, so, nothing daunted, the authorities decided to dye them black, and add a token grey button. At least this kind of difficulty has not worried their 20th-century successors. In everything the eight merchants were closely involved, and it was they who drew up the Scheme, before the school opened, to give form to their ideas. They recognised in this that for a school to succeed it would be 'absolutely necessary that the Scholars be kept under good Discipline and Subjection'. At the same time, this was to be no over-harsh regime, for the Master was, in the words of that first Scheme, to 'study and indeavour to win the love and affection of the Children, thereby to invite them and encourage them rather than by correction to force them to learne'. Is it fanciful to see here the seeds of the easy relationships between staff and pupils which have characterised the modern schools over the years?

It was not only for the scholars that the desired 'good Discipline' was to be demanded, for the eight founders were equally strict about themselves. They would readily have accepted as perfectly natural the requirement made by an early benefactor that they must themselves all live 'a very good and exemplary life', and they clearly took their duties very seriously. Each had to sign a ruling whereby he accepted the need for concentration of 'the Businesse of the Hospitall', and agreed that anything else risked the imposition of a fine of sixpence for a first offence, 12 pence for a second, and 18 pence for a third. They also undertook to pay a fine of twopence if they were late for a meeting, or absent without good reason. Perhaps these precautions were unnecessary, for they all took a personal interest in the boys at their school and wished to examine their progress. At first, each took charge of five boys out of the 40 but there were pitfalls—could it be that dealings in 'sope and candles', for example, did not necessarily make an adequate basis for detailed examination of the Catechism or of mathematical principles? Instead, the eight decided to see in turn as many boys as possible, and as a group ask them questions.

In their suggestions to the first Master they appointed, the Founders showed their wish to temper the demands on the boys they were caring for by adding some form of treat at times. On the very first day of the school, the children's official attendance at their parish church of St Margaret's, Westminster, meant a long sermon to them and their parents. So it was arranged that after the service they should be fed, and a sentence in the Minutes speaks of their 'dinner at Hell in Pallace Yard', a little startling without the knowledge that a coffee-house near Westminster Hall was called Hell. Had they known of it, the children would surely have approved of the allocation of the three pounds allowed for the day, with one pound for the sermon and two pounds for the food. Once the annual processions of

Charity Children to St Andrew's Church in Holborn were organised, the Grey Coat children always took part, and they were provided 'for their comfort on their way home' with £12 of gingerbread to be divided among them—with very strict instructions that it was not to be eaten in church. The Gingerbread Services, as they were called, continued until 1877, and their successors must be the Foundation Services in Westminster Abbey which are periodically enjoyed now by the two schools on the Foundation.

During those early years, at every turn there were those eight Founders, thoroughly involved in their project, and proving to be very human and thoughtful people. They also had the good sense to think of the future. No one would suggest that they even dreamed of the day when Queen Anne's opened in Caversham, but they certainly tackled the need they found for the expansion of their charity into a firmly based Foundation from which the boarding school in the country would later develop. Their school outgrew the house in Broad Sanctuary and, again on 6 January, this time in 1701, it moved to the site of the present Grey Coat Hospital. It is at this time that there begins the link with Westminster Abbey, still so much cherished by the two schools. A Poorhouse in Totthill Fields, no longer large enough for its purpose, occupied ground rented from the Dean and Chapter, and this was in turn acquired by the Foundation. The property included not only the old buildings but also a considerable amount of ground, some of it since used for extended school buildings and some known as Grey Coat Gardens and Grey Coat Buildings. The front of the main school building is still the same as it was, with the turret for the clock presented by Thomas Wisdome. Round the Board Room table, bought at this time, the progress of Grey Coat Hospital, and later of Queen Anne's also, has been debated. The 12 chairs and footstools are still there, but succeeding generations of governors have cause to be grateful to Mr. Ffyler for the efficient way he managed to 'obtain something to destroy Buggs in the Trustees Room'.

With their school moving its premises and expanding, the Founders were once more very busily involved. They met nearly every day, and concerned themselves with the making of

1. Frontage of the Grey Coat Hospital.

bedsteads, they employed women specially to make the bedding, and for each bed they provided 'rugges and a kiverlid'. It would be easy to look on some of their provisions and detailed care for the life of the children in their schools as both niggling and almost naive, but it was not so. It was a measure of their genuine interest and their realistic understanding of human shortcomings. The exact details of weights, amounts, etc., for food, for example, and their interest in the details of the provision of a copper for brewing and for washing, may seem rather lowly concerns for a governing body, but they were justified a century later when there were riots at the Hospital over very poor living conditions and semi-starvation. It is good to know that the governors of that time responded as generously and sensibly as the old Founders would have done; and eventually the improvements they made were so good that the Hospital could again 'rank among the first of its kind'—though instructions for the use of that copper in 1701 might well have been useful even as late as 1874 when the girls' black petticoats descended from child to child and were never washed.

Money was a real problem, and continued to be so. There were benefactors who helped, and gifts which ranged from £67 of mutton to 'one hundred sticht books, intituled *Prayers for the Ignorent*, to be given to the children when bound'. Unfortunately, promises of support were not always honoured, and staff at the London Office now faced with a few recalcitrant feepayers may like to spare a thought for those eight merchants, six of whom in rotation spent each weekly meeting time visiting those who had promised support but not paid up, while the remaining two and the steward dealt with the business of the meeting. Two Grey Coat boys were regularly seen in the City, with some of the governors attempting to gain financial support, and the wands they carried were later kept in the Grey Coat Hospital after it became a girls' school. But benefactors there certainly were, and some of them are remembered by portraits which used to hang in the Board Room in the Hospital and are now in the Assembly Hall there. One of these was Mr. Charles Twitty who left the Foundation £500, a considerable sum in those days. Since his executors would not hand over the legacy without a seal, he was indirectly responsible for the Foundation Seal, so much a part of the inheritance of the present schools—though the inscription on it, 'God Give The Increase', was not intended to be called into use in quite the way suggested by a sad recipient of a letter announcing a fee increase at Queen Anne's about 260 years later. Sometimes legacies were hard to come by, and it is said that part of one is still owing today nearly three centuries later. Years afterwards, the ghost of Richard Ffyler must have haunted the Hospital that was partly his creation since only one third of his legacy to it ever reached the Foundation. Whatever the difficulties the Founders

2. God give the increase.

encountered during those early years, they never gave up, and they never lost sight of their aims for their school, both for the children and for the adults. When the time came for a steward to be appointed, their first requirement was for 'a person honest and faithfull and of a sober life', and only after that was he expected to be 'one that understandeth accompts'. It is sad that their first appointment failed because he was 'too ancient and not sufficiently exact', and that the second proved to be a crook.

The Founders had tried to awaken Queen Anne's generosity and gain a share in her Bounty by arranging a sermon to be preached before her, with special reference to the Grey Coat children. The result was not quite what they expected, for instead of the hoped-for financial contribution, they received the names of two children who would, the Queen said, benefit from places in the Hospital. They must surely have accepted those two, for their request for royal recognition of their charity was answered by the granting of a royal charter in 1706. With Thomas Wisdome now officially appointed treasurer, and Samuel Michell as secretary, the small parochial charity of 1698 had become within eight years the Royal Foundation of Queen Anne in Westminster, a title both schools today use with much pride. The Queen's portrait hangs in the Grey Coat Hospital, and an excellent copy of it is in the school which honours her name.

During the 18th century the Foundation grew and in many ways prospered, though living conditions for the children were austere. In 1738, an inventory gave the number of beds for one hundred children as 49, and there were only eight chairs available for the whole school. Food and drink were subject to rigorous financial restraints. But the foundation was generally well-supported, with well-known people such as Sir Robert Walpole among the benefactors. Arrangements by the governors for the children within the Hospital still showed their care for them, and their insistence on the best they could do for them. When the time came for the children to become apprentices, exhaustive inquiries were made and very careful investigations, to make sure the final choice was right, and the boys and girls went off to their apprenticeships supplied with a full range of clothing. The story of Mr. and Mrs. Pippit illustrates the governors' determination that the interests of the children came first. These two wished to adopt a child at the Hospital, but the governors insisted that she must to begin with go for a month's trial, to make sure that she liked living with them and was happy. The enthusiastic involvement of the eight Founders still lived on with their successors.

Unhappily, by the later part of the 18th century, trouble was brewing in all endowed charity schools, and the Hospital was not immune. An infirmary nurse at Grey Coat was murdered by a boy from Christ's Hospital; dissatisfied children at the Hospital threw hot coals at their Master in protest against their living conditions and the lack of good food; even after a replacement Head Master and some improvements, the children as late as 1867 staged their Great Rebellion which produced many changes. With all this unrest and continued troubles, it is not surprising that a Commission was set up in 1869 to look into the affairs of all Endowed Schools, including of course the Royal Foundation of Queen Anne in Westminster. It is from the results of this Commission that Queen Anne's School was established in Caversham.

The Commissioners recognised that Westminster had seen many changes over nearly 200 years, and that for most children day schools had become more appropriate than boarding schools. They also set to work to sort out all the various charities and foundations which were attempting to educate the City's children. It was 1870 which saw the beginning of state education for all children, and naturally this had an impact. The Commissioners recognised the changing ethos of the time, with 'a greater disposition to accept nothing as a favour which can be claimed as a right'. They argued the merits of fee-paying, coupled with generous provision for free places, and decided to sort out the mixed Grey Coat Hospital by sending the boys to other Endowed Schools, and establishing the Grey Coat Hospital as a day school for 300 girls. The governors were not entirely in favour of such changes. They were very conscious of the charitable basis of the Foundation, nor did they relish the Commissioners' insistence on the need for women governors, particularly for girls' schools. But they lost the argument, and in 1872 reluctantly accepted a new Scheme for the Foundation. Two years later, the re-organised day school opened. With all its well-established Westminster links, it was fitting that, on the Sunday before the opening, prayers were said in neighbouring churches with a special petition: 'That it may please God to give to the children the spirit of Reverence and Obedience, and to those set over them Wisdom and Holy Fear'. Twenty years later, the same words were used for the opening of Queen Anne's School.

The Scheme agreed between the Commissioners and the governors of the Foundation required the establishment of a boarding school not far from London. The fees were to be sufficiently high to cover expenses, and the governors tried to safeguard the Westminster connection by insisting on a large proportion of children from there. They were very well aware that the poorer children in the city had inherited the right to the free education the Foundation had offered; but the practical difficulties were obvious, for how, at a boarding school, would richer children from more privileged homes live and work easily with the late 19th-century representatives of the original Founders' 'greatest objects of charity' they could find? The governors agonised over their awareness of their responsibilities and the new demands being made on them, and finally resolved their problems by saying that Westminster children wishing to attend the boarding school would have to have three years at the Foundation's day school first, and only move to the boarding school with the approval of their Headmistress. It seems fairly certain that the eight merchants at the beginning would have been themselves more closely involved, but perhaps by this time this was a sensible compromise.

So the way was at last clear for the new school. After all their difficulties, good fortune smiled on these governors, for out at Caversham, on what the Minute Books refer to as 'a piece of rising ground in the country', there were the buildings and grounds that had been used by 'a school for young gentlemen', called Amersham Hall. This was now up for sale. It had been a Baptist school, founded by Ebenezer West in 1824, and later run by his son Alfred. The initials in the stonework of the fireplace in the present school dining-hall still recall them. The Wests had not admitted any day boys, and there had been 80 boarders. It was spoken of as a 'very happy and well-ordered establishment', and perhaps part of the inheritance enjoyed by the girls was that happiness, for over the years it has always characterised the new school. In 1893, the Foundation's purchase from Amersham Hall was completed, and by the following summer Queen Anne's School was opened, on the Royal Foundation of Queen Anne in Westminster.

Chapter II
The First Headmistress
Miss Holmes (1894-1917)

Faith had been at the root of all that had been achieved by the Foundation: faith in the future, faith in the essential goodness of people, and, above all, faith in Christian principles. The opening of Queen Anne's on Ascension Day, 1894, was yet another example of this faith. Miss Holmes had been the headmistress of the Graham Street Francis Holland School, but she was persuaded by Archdeacon Furse to leave there and take on the task of leading this new Caversham school. The Archdeacon backed his choice of headmistress by sending her his daughter Katherine, considered by many in those early days to be one of the most influential members of the fledgling Queen Anne's. Miss Holmes was fortunate in the girls who came with her from Graham Street. Their relations with her were excellent, and they were as determined as she was to make a success of this new school. Nor should the trust in her shown by their parents be forgotten.

Down in Caversham no one had any experience of boarding school life, and the story goes that on the first Saturday the Headmistress, her staff and some senior girls all went off to Reading to see the shops, leaving the remaining children to their own devices. Perhaps this sowed the seed of the spirit of independence and self-reliance which has characterised the school over the years. By the following Monday, school was to begin in earnest. Furnished with the stationery and the books they needed, the girls assembled in their classrooms, only to discover that all the desks, left behind from Amersham Hall, were locked. Hodges, the porter and general handyman, had worked in the old boys' school, and he quickly proved to be as essential to this new school as so many of his successors have been. When appealed to, he produced well over a hundred keys, no labels on any of them. So the morning was spent by everyone in an attempt to unlock the desks needed for the girls, after which the keys were thankfully abandoned for ever.

The Grey Coat Hospital in London had always worked under a Scheme of Education, amended at various times over the years. In the Scheme of 1873, updated in 1894, certain definite guide lines were laid down for the new boarding school. Tuition fees were to be not more than £5 or less than £3 a year. Boarding fees, the Scheme states, 'shall be as low as the Governors can fix ... and shall be calculated to cover the cost, but shall not exceed £20 a year'. The Governors' careful and well-informed probing into any fee increase so many decades later has a good precedent. Queen Anne's was never intended to be for the very rich but, in the words of the 1894 Scheme, for 'girls who are of good

3.   The first 38 girls.

character and of sufficient bodily health'. The entrance fee for each girl was to be ten shillings, a sum which, despite the changing value of money, remained the same for well over 60 years. The subjects taught were to include Religious Instruction, the three R's, Domestic Science, French and 'at least one branch of Natural Science'. Latin and German could be added to this list. The girls were officially expected to leave at the age of 15, but were allowed to stay on by recommendation to the governors. Those girls, who from the very beginning formed themselves into a band of prefects prepared to undertake the supervision of younger pupils out of school hours, were themselves very young for their responsibilities. But the system worked. The layout of School House, the oldest part of the buildings, has always made over-careful supervision very difficult, if not impossible, and so was further re-inforced the spirit of independence which scorned any suggestion of vicarious nannying.

During the first four years at Caversham, some building was undertaken. The gym and the gym classrooms wing were built, which explains the curious title of New Wing dormitories for what has now for some years been part of Boulte House. Then in 1898, 200 years after the very beginning of the Foundation in Westminster, the Foundation Stone for a school chapel was laid by the past Chairman of the Governors, Mr. George A. Spottiswoode. With the dedication of that Chapel in January the following year, the heart of Queen Anne's was firmly in place. In his address that day the Bishop of Oxford said he hoped the Chapel would become the centre of the life of the school, and a true source of inspiration. So down the years it has always proved to be. *The Chronicle*, that useful school barometer, in those early days never failed to report in full addresses given at Confirmation Services and at other important events. Until comparatively recently Speech Days or Prize Givings always began with a service in Chapel for the school and the visitors, and the practice was discontinued only because sheer pressure of numbers made it completely impossible.

When it was first opened, the Chapel received many very generous gifts. Miss Elsie Day, then headmistress of the Grey Coat Hospital, the Foundation's London day school, used to say that she and her school looked upon Queen Anne's as a younger sister; so it is not surprising to find her parents contributing gold and silver medals and a silver cup, which were all transformed into Communion silver at the expense of Miss Day and her school. Included in those donors were a number of men who had known the Grey Coat Hospital before the new scheme was in operation—the last Headmaster, the Usher, the Organist and a number of men who had been educated there. Yet another link with the Foundation and its history was emphasised in this way. Many of the furnishings of the early Chapel still remain. In the ante-chapel a glass case now holds the Lectern Bible given by Miss Day, showing both the Victorian love of symbolism and the old days of the Foundation: the cover of the Bible was made from a beam from the original Grey Coat Hospital, with a cross on the cover made from Bulgarian silver, a Spanish silver clasp and

4.   The prefects, 1900.

5.   Laying the foundation stone of the Chapel.

with the corners of the cover clamped in Dutch silver, the silver symbolising, therefore, the union of Christendom throughout Europe. An oak lectern was given by one of the governors. Almost immediately after the dedication of the Chapel, an organ fund was started by a member of the staff of Queen Anne's, and by 1900 the organ was in place and has been in constant use ever since.

Miss Holmes wanted the Chapel to be as beautiful as possible. At first all the windows were plain glass, but in 1903 she started a fund for a stained glass East Window. This she wanted to be designed and executed by the well-known and much admired Victorian artist in glass, C. E. Kempe. It proved to be an expensive business, but led by her the school set to work to raise the money, and three years later the window was dedicated. There is the Westminster connection for all to see: the royal coat-of-arms for the Royal Grey Coat Foundation of Queen Anne; the arms of Edward the Confessor, the founder of Westminster Abbey; St Peter, to whom the Abbey is dedicated; St Margaret of Antioch, the Patron Saint of St Margaret's, Westminster, the church used for many years by the Grey Coat children in Westminster. The sharp-eyed can see in the glass the 'signature' of Kempe, a stook of corn. The following year two more Kempe windows were added on the south side of the sanctuary; one of these, the Founders' Window, was given by Miss Day and the London Grey Coat Hospital, and the other by Miss Holmes and Queen Anne's School. They form a pair, just as the two schools were working side by side. The interest of local residents in Caversham and their support for the school were shown by an altar cross, given in memory of General Radcliffe by his wife and two daughters. In the centre was a cross formed by amethysts from a brooch he had given Mrs. Radcliffe. He and his family frequently attended School Chapel, and the altar cross, which was in use until the recent reorganisation of the sanctuary, not only showed the local support the school has always enjoyed, but also fitted well with the beauty of the Chapel for which Miss Holmes was always seeking. Another early gift to the Chapel was the Sanctuary Lamp, known affectionately to generations of girls as 'Twink'. There is a story that this lamp was originally black, but zealous cleaning on one occasion removed the coating and revealed it as silver to the consternation of all, not least the over-enthusiastic cleaner. The lamp was known and loved by the school for many, many years, until the building of the Choir Gallery meant that it interfered with the view of the altar from there. So many of the Chapel's furnishings, both now and from the past, reveal the school's history and commemorate those who have been able to serve there. For instance, there is the Chapel bell which was cast and hung in memory of Miss Mackarness, who was in charge of one of the outside boarding houses. Its use to summon all girls to Chapel seems a very suitable memorial for one whose attitude to her house was said to be sane and unsentimental, and who insisted that members of all the early outside houses were very much an integral part of the school.

With a headmistress, her staff and her pupils, all with little or no idea of boarding school life, the governors, and particularly the Chairman of those governors, had much to do with the shaping of the school. In the very early days, Mr. George Spottiswoode, who was in office from 1879-1884, had a strong influence on the way Queen Anne's developed, and it is certainly right that his name is on the stone commemorating the foundation of the Chapel. When he died in 1899 it was said of him as Chairman that his power was 'due to his capacity for worship', and he must have been a quiet source of strength to Miss Holmes. Perhaps, he lacked the dogged determination of some holders of such a position, and indeed one of his fellow governors said of him that he was 'too holy a man to be a good chairman'. What is certain is that everything we know of him from the records of that time points to his having been what his own generation would recognise as an ideal Christian gentleman. He set the pattern not only for the strong emphasis at Queen Anne's on Christian values, but also for the quiet trust and confident bond between him and the Headmistress. Prebendary Northcote, a later Chairman of the Greycoat Foundation, showed the same devoted interest in his turn when, on the occasion of the dedication of the windows on the south side of the Sanctuary, he took the opportunity of explaining to the girls the significance of the Founders' Window and its thankful remembrance of the eight men whose names are listed there, and also showing the connection with the Epiphany, the day on which began the Grey Coat Hospital Foundation. At Easter too the Chapel was a place of happiness as the school celebrated the Resurrection, the heart of the Christian faith; for the dating of school terms then meant that Easter was very often enjoyed at school, and was always a joyful occasion. Those early Chairmen would have approved.

A hundred years ago expectations from girls' schools were very different, and the idea that girls as well as boys deserved a thorough education was slow to take root. The choice of subjects in the 1894 Scheme was sound, but by today's standards very limited. Examination systems were in their infancy, and the official leaving age at Queen Anne's of 15 cannot have helped. But there were some national examinations available, and the very first issue of *The Chronicle* mentions some successes in The Higher Certificate of The Oxford and Cambridge Board. The numbers in the school increased very satisfactorily, and eight years after the opening it was recorded that there were 141 girls present at the Prize Giving, held in the Dining Hall after a Chapel Service. In time the numbers became too large for this or for the gym, and the speeches and actual presentation of prizes were transferred to the field where a platform and some seating were arranged in front of the pavilion. The English climate must sometimes have caused problems, but Miss Holmes and her school never considered difficulties, always using to the best advantage whatever was available.

Standards of education were beginning to rise everywhere, and in 1906 Queen Anne's had its first important General Inspection. At that time, the Head of School was Cara Gascoigne, later to teach games at her old school, and become housemistress of Ffyler. The Chief Inspector was a Dr. Scott, and afterwards he sent a book to Cara in recognition of the 'good word and good tone' he had found. The school may not have been what would nowadays be called mainly academic, but clearly it was holding its own when judged according to the demands of the time. There were certainly many differences in the kind of preparation for adult life which was to be given to boys from that given to girls. Two years after the General Inspection at a Prize Giving, the visiting speaker, Mrs. Baillie Reynolds, said that if there were any difference in the mission of men and women, it was that women were intended to make people enjoy life. Surely an endorsement of width of education for girls, rather than any narrower concept of specialised training.

Changes were, however, in the air, and the academic side of the life of Queen Anne's gradually became more important. Regular Mark Readings, familiar to countless generations of girls since those earlier days, were an accepted part of the routine. More external examinations were successfully taken. Any form of higher education for women was considered very exceptional, and there was extremely little provision for it; but Queen Anne's was ready to take what opportunities there were. The first report of an Oxbridge scholarship was of one for Modern Languages awarded to Madge Sopwith by Lady Margaret Hall, the Oxford College of which she later became Vice-Principal. In 1913, the fourth Oxford Scholarship was gained; and those who find distasteful the low place of Latin in the 1894 Scheme as a subject which 'may be added', will appreciate the fact that this scholarship was awarded for Classics. The previous year, the school had performed its first Latin play, which was based on selections from the Aeneid dealing with the story of Dido and Aeneas. By now, school life was no mere polishing of a few accomplishments, and the prize for Greek Testament, which still exists, was given in Miss Holmes' time by one of the governors, Miss Ireland Blackburne, later to become Chairman of the Queen Anne's Governors. Everything suggests that the Headmistress' aim was to develop the talents and skills of her pupils in whatever way best suited them, academic or not.

6.   Miss Holmes and the prefects, 1906.

The social side of the school life and the demands of the time on all women were certainly not forgotten. There were frequent musical evenings and concerts from the very beginning. The staff always took a large part in these, as indeed they did in all the activities that went on. The concept of an evening devoted to music would be very familiar to all Victorian and Edwardian families, who were used to providing their own entertainment. The children in the family were expected both to listen and to contribute. At Queen Anne's these musical evenings were largely provided by the teachers of music with perhaps some of the more gifted and advanced pupils. There was much singing as well as instrumental playing. By 1911 these evenings were becoming more carefully organised and each month was devoted to a special composer. The first of the weekly evenings would be given over to a short account of his life, and the remaining musical evenings would consist of performances by the music staff of his work, both instrumental and choral. No girl leaving Queen Anne's would lack a certain amount of basic musical knowledge and some appreciation, as would, of course, be expected of her at that time. There were also regular

7.   The first staff.

concerts or social evenings at the end of each term, open to outside visitors. These were provided by both staff and girls and included solos as well as some orchestral playing. The place of music teachers in the school orchestra has a long history. As well as musical items there was usually some recitation, possibly in French and German.

Music was not the only enjoyment open to the girls. Progressive whist parties were held frequently, with staff participation, and there were various clubs formed to develop interests. One of these was the Field Club. The members would take a train to some nearby station, and then walk. They were expected to collect wild flowers from which to study Botany, and they sketched. These expeditions took place quite frequently, and the comparative freedom the girls could enjoy in those gentler and safer times might well be the envy of their present-day successors. The Field Club was for those especially interested, but the whole school, of course, enjoyed the traditional picnic on Ascension Day, the school's birthday, and this continued until comparatively recently. There was another early and very lively group, the History Club. Caversham was quite well placed for interesting visits, and Windsor was a regular destination. Also, there were lectures from prominent experts of the day, and sometimes an exhibition of a particular skill. For example, in 1906 the school saw an exhibition of water divining. This was not considered an unqualified success as it seemed to prove the existence of a torrent under the front lawn. Over 50 years later, when the legend of a large lake of water under the quadrangle was found to be no legend but sober fact, with some exit for water below the front lawn, the scepticism which the water-diviner endured seems sadly unjustified.

One of the strange groups dating right back to 1898 was the School Fire Brigade. This started in two sections: one was for the firemen, who were five members of staff and 15 girls; the other consisted of six members of staff and five girls who were 'set apart to prevent disorder throughout the school'—no seen-and-not-heard Victorian children at Queen Anne's, it would seem. All went well to begin with, and the practices were reported as showing 'the spirit of promptness and activity'. The following year the numbers in the Brigade increased as they were given more buckets, but at a later practice some of them did not appear at all. After this, efficiency deteriorated, and scorn is poured on the workers of the pumps and 'the excellent work they would have done had they had the pumps acting'. Nor was this all, for the hose-holders were castigated for having aimed the water at the other members of the Brigade, 'so making sure that whatever else should catch fire they at least should be spared—a most thoughtful and considerate idea, but I think it would be wiser to devote all energies on the actual fire'. After this public report, it seems surprising that the Fire Brigade recruited any members, but somehow or other it survived until the late 1950s when, as a final blow to its pride or usefulness, it was discovered that by then the hoses did not fit the hydrants. The Brigade was disbanded and this odd mixture of would-be efficiency and farce came to an end.

There were official Half Term holidays, but usually only one day was allowed. Some of the girls went out with family or friends, but entertainments were devised for those left behind, and the staff did their best to make the day a happy one. Many of the girls took the opportunity to go for long walks into the country. There was often a match arranged for those who were games-minded, with a more frivolous division into teams, such as supporters of Oxford or Cambridge, chocolate lovers or toffee eaters, Army connections or Navy, and so on. There might well be a special concert or a staff entertainment for the girls, and sometimes a dance was organised. In all this, the staff were very active and as generous with their time as always. It would probably not have occurred to them to be otherwise, for together they and their pupils were one community. With the different term dates, Easter at school was a weekend of celebrations after the austere observance of Lent. Sunday was naturally devoted to joyful services in a chapel filled with flowers, and by Monday the more secular occupation of an egg-finding competition could be enjoyed. The staff often provided an entertainment that evening, including one year an adaptation of Hilaire Belloc's *Cautionary Tales*, that perennial stand-by in so many schools over the years for a quick-fire staff entertainment. Everything was done to keep the girls happily occupied and amused.

The finances of the school were a problem from the very beginning. As part of the Grey Coat Hospital Foundation, Queen Anne's came under the Charity Commissioners and a close watch was kept on all expenditure. The ever-green topic of school food reared its head early, and there were those who thought too much economy was practised. At one time the hymn 'New Every Morning' was sung in Chapel very frequently, until it was discovered that the line 'the sparing use of daily food' had become a catchword among the girls and the use of that hymn was then rapidly discontinued. It is probably true that one of the least important things in assessing any school is its buildings, but for all there have to be changes; and increased numbers, new emphases in educational theory, new expectations from society at different times, all have their importance and are translated into bricks and mortar. The first essential buildings of the gymnasium and gym classrooms rapidly became inadequate for the growing school. In 1902 came the dedication of the West Wing, with its classrooms, dormitories and sitting rooms—no new building then was merely opened, but it was dedicated for its purpose in a Christian-orientated community. To begin with Miss Holmes had lived in the front of the school, but the West Wing was designed to provide her with a bedroom and sitting-room at its west end. Here she lived for four years until The Cottage was specially built for her. She then had a house which was self-contained and large enough to permit entertaining, but at the same time providing immediate and easy access to the rest of the school, an ideal situation for her. In her rooms in the West Wing she had had electric light, unlike most of the rest of the school which was gas-lit. At the end of the 1950s, there was an electricity failure which, oddly, applied both to The Cottage and to the end of the West Wing. Subsequent investigations showed that electricity had been brought for Miss Holmes from the West Wing to The Cottage by means of a thin wire which was sunk, at no great depth, in the garden between the two, near the large cherry tree that is there now. Horror and relief mingled when possible consequences to digging gardeners were considered. No doubt those eight old Founders had kept everyone safe.

Two years later, more classrooms were added. A good sized studio was built, and continued to be used for Art until a new building for Art and Craft followed the demolition of the old Swimmer, and then it became a classroom for one of the Sixth Forms. Next to it was a botanical greenhouse, still showing signs of its early use with the curiously coiled pipes. The Craft Room was given as much light as possible by extra windows into the corridor, and it was known as the Glass Cage for many years. Until comparatively recently, it contained a sink which had been needed for craft work. With all this building and a growing number of celebrations, the provision of a Union Jack and flagstaff seemed very fitting. This was placed in the shrubbery opposite the front door, where it remained for many years until it fell victim in the 1960s to a road-widening scheme.

As the school grew, so inevitably did the problems. It is difficult for those of us who have known Queen Anne's as a close-knit community to appreciate fully some of the early struggles for Miss Holmes as she tried to achieve her ideal of one family, something she most successfully passed on to future generations. The numbers of boarders increased, and the day girls were in danger of feeling they were there on sufferance, rather than being an integral part of the school. Perhaps the change in afternoon school hours made at this time was seen to be favouring the boarders who would more easily take to afternoon games, with tea at 3.45 p.m., and then prep. and occasional lessons for three hours until Chapel and supper. Miss Holmes recognised the problem of possible division and did her best to put it right. In an issue of *The Chronicle* in 1909 she wrote a special letter to her day girls in an attempt to stress their important contribution to the school. This, it seems, was not a complete success, and so she decided to abolish the use of the words 'Day Girls'. In future, these girls were to be known as 'Amersham House', a reference to the earlier

8. Miss Holmes

school on the same site, and this continued for some years. The organisation of the school meant that even the boarders were not completely united, and in practice the school was split into three: first came School House, the heart of the school, now the home of Boulte and Wisdome; then there were the outside boarding houses in Caversham, run independently of the main school, each arranging its own fees for boarding, and of those known to Miss Holmes only Hillside now remains part of the school; the third section of the school was the Day Girls' House, by 1910 known as Amersham. The divisions were clearly recognised, and even underlined in games competitions, for the outside boarding houses competed amongst themselves for their own trophies in lacrosse, tennis and cricket. It needed both a geographical upheaval and the imaginative linking together of inside and outside houses many years later to get rid of those divisions.

The problems were there, but the early records make it clear that at the centre of everything was Miss Holmes, always involved with new ideas and developments. The strain on her must have been almost unbearable at times, and she richly deserved her six months away from the school in 1905. She must have enjoyed her welcome back by all the girls, dressed in Queen Anne's red. Five years later her health was obviously suffering and she had to be away from her work again; but she had shown herself to be good at delegating, and everything went on smoothly in her absence. In November 1912 she was once again given some months off and this time she went to India for a complete rest and change. Her return to Queen Anne's just before Easter was affectionate and very enthusiastic: the school was waiting for her that evening, with no thought of such mundane matters as normal bed-times, and the girls gave her a rousing welcome from their perches on the front stairs and from the front hall; the welcome was accompanied by the playing of handbells, a new skill taught to the Sixth Form by the Chaplain at that time, the Rev. C. D. Jenkyn, himself a bell-ringer of considerable talent, and well-known in Oxfordshire. Miss Holmes had come back to her school, and from then until she retired at the end of 1917 her time and all her thoughts were once more devoted to Queen Anne's.

From the very beginning games have always been important. The second term, with the numbers of girls almost doubled, saw the arrival of some new members of staff, among them Miss Balzani. Her name may not be known to all the present school but her achievements have certainly had a lasting effect. She was a linguist and taught French, but it is her enthusiasm for games which has had a lasting impact. When she first came the usual unit for any team games was the form, but Miss Balzani decided that the girls should play in clubs instead. The most proficient girls were to be in a Savoyard Club, a reference to her favourite part of France. Next came the Orions, named for her favourite constellation. The younger, less able children, were to be called Cats and Mice. This system of Clubs is still very much alive, and the keystone of the organisation of games. Miss Balzani started each section with its own Captain, Secretary and Treasurer, and for the Savs., as the Savoyards were known, these officials were at first members of staff, Miss Balzani herself being the Captain. A few girls were eventually allowed on the Committee, and gradually they took over. The clubs were used for all three games of tennis, cricket and hockey, for it was some years later that the winter game was changed to lacrosse. The

9. First Savs.

Savs. had a special uniform of a green skirt—fairly short for that time—and a white blouse with a striped tie. A badge for the 1st hockey XI was added in 1901.

The hockey Savs. commanded much attention. Four members of the staff were included in the team in 1896 when their first match was played at Queen Anne's against Miss Holmes' former school in Graham Street; and, with Miss Balzani one of the four, no doubt they helped Queen Anne's to their 6-0 victory. The following spring the first recorded match against Wycombe Abbey, with a team including five members of staff, resulted in another victory for Queen Anne's. Whether or not there were complaints from other schools is not known, but six months later it was decided that for matches against other schools the teams would be drawn from girls only, though members of staff continued to play with the girls for matches against clubs. Certainly the hockey teams met with great success, and four years after the arrival of Miss Balzani at Queen Anne's the Savs. in one season won 14 out of their 15 matches, and the odd one out was drawn. In the first nine years of organised hockey Queen Anne's lost only seven matches out of 61, and was reportedly known in Germany then because it was 'the school that played hockey so well'.

Once the *Chronicle* came into existence in 1898 it always included detailed accounts of each club and of the progress of its members. These reports were frequently decidedly critical in tone, despite so much success, and this was especially true of tennis and cricket. Among the tennis players there was little approval for 'some girls who never play except in their ties, so that they don't make much improvement'. Even advances in cricket in the standard of batting are mentioned in such a way as to suggest earlier, grave shortcomings, for the improvement is beacuse 'a good many girls have got more idea of defending their wicket'. Poor attempts at any game were clearly not acceptable.

Miss Balzani was herself an excellent swimmer, and the old boys' school swimming bath was used to the full. Queen Anne's was fortunate in having inherited this asset from Amersham. Though it was said that the girls had to learn to dive in a special way because the bath was so shallow, dive they certainly did and the bath was in use until it was replaced over 60 years later. As early as 1898 there was a silver medal given each year for the champion swimmer, and a prize for diving. The emptying of the swimming bath must have strained to their limits the excellent relationships which existed between the school and Caversham residents as the water made its way across the school's ground on the opposite side of the road and flooded into their houses at the bottom of the rise. Gymnastics, too, felt the benefit of Miss Balzani's expertise and enthusiasm. More apparatus was purchased and the new gymnasium welcomed. The dress for gymnastics was always scarlet, and the emphasis was on exercises, known as drill. One of the most long-lasting activities of the school dates from 1898. The girls were divided into five sections, with an additional group for the day girls. Five girls from the top section were put in charge of these sections as sergeants to drill their groups each morning, and help with afternoon classes. It all sounds strange to the present day, but it seems to have been enjoyed since on one occasion a special drill session in the quadrangle was organised as a half-term treat. At first the whole activity was known as Sections, but was later called Sergeants, and as such continued right into the 1950s. Perhaps, as so often happens, everyone was so used to it that its usefulness was never questioned. One prize, still given each year, recalls the recognition of a high standard in all matters athletic, and also provides a good link with the past. The prize was funded by Russell Spokes, himself an old boy of Amersham Hall who had become a governor of the Grey Coat Hospital Foundation. He established a fund to provide a prize each year for athletic performance by a Queen Anne's girl. It was to be of not more than £1, but for about the last 35 years has been subsidised further.

The inspiration and enthusiasm of Miss Balzani set the games at Queen Anne's on a firm foundation, and it might well be thought that the school had had its share of good fortune. This was not so, and another outstanding games mistress followed her, Miss Newbold, whose name is still linked to some of the tennis courts enjoyed by the present school. It was during her time that the switch was made from hockey to lacrosse. There had been a brief, abortive attempt in 1904, but the school returned to hockey for two more seasons. By 1907 the upper school was playing lacrosse, though the juniors were still enjoying hockey. There was even a cautious beginning at lacrosse matches when the Savs. played Wycombe Abbey's 3rd XII and lost 2-3. Not surprisingly the team benefited from some coaching afterwards from a former Wycombe Abbey captain, and lacrosse continued. There were some strange events connected with this progress. For instance, there is a record of a match against a mixed Winchester team, who, we are told, played

10.   'Sergeants'.

the old game, while Queen Anne's played the Canadian game, and won 13-1. Even in an earlier hockey match, Queen Anne's victory over St Katherine's, Wantage, was noted with the comment that 'the Wantage team played a slightly different game from that which we play'. In games, it seems, variety was all. Gradually, lacrosse was firmly established as the winter game for everyone, and it was on the excellent foundation laid by Miss Newbold that the school's outstanding reputation for lacrosse was built, a reputation which has lasted over all the years and is still very much alive today.

Match practice for the girls was considered very important, and as well as competitive games within the clubs, Miss Newbold wanted more games tournaments. This was in no way the more modern conception of Houses, but simply a useful division, only for games.

These Houses were called after the eight original founders of 1698, and each had its own colour which was shown on the sleeves of the gym dresses. The Savs. were divided fairly between the eight Houses. With all the earlier emphasis on games it was perhaps fitting that the division of the school into Houses, for so many years now such a fundamental part of Queen Anne's, was foreshadowed by Miss Newbold's idea of an expedient division of the girls on the games field. The Houses were used not only for lacrosse but also for tennis and cricket, though the standards reached in these two games do not seem to have been high. At one time a professional cricket player was engaged to coach some of the girls, but he became known not for his coaching expertise but for his constant exhortation, ''it it 'ard, Miss, do 'it it 'ard'. The general level of play cannot have been very inspiring, for the story goes that a foreman on a building site overlooking the field was heard to threaten one of his workman by saying, 'If you don't work a bit harder, you will come back here this afternoon to watch those girls playing cricket'. Tennis and cricket belonged to the summer, but it was lacrosse that mattered.

It was certainly not only games which bound the school together. Miss Holmes was intent on starting a community, never an institution, and to her the girls who had left her care were still part of the extended family. Only four years after the opening of Queen Anne's, a society was formed to keep them all together. It was called the Old Girls' Society at first, but Miss Holmes stated that this was only 'for want of some better title', and she invited suggestions for a name. Apparently none was forthcoming, or none considered suitable, so The Old Girls' Society it has remained. Her ideas for this new branch of the community provide an interesting sidelight on her ideals for her school and her faith in the essential goodness of people. She wrote, 'There are no rules to keep, we only want love and loyalty amongst ourselves, and out of these will of necessity grow a desire to do something for others less fortunate than ourselves'. Her simple belief in her pupils may strike some as naive, but surely also refreshingly optimistic.

It was decided that there should be a meeting of this new society each year on the Saturday nearest to Ascension Day. At the very first meeting the Old Girls discovered, as had countless folk before them, that any collection of human beings needs some regulation, and a committee was formed to decide on rules for the society. The importance of the Old Girls in the young school was emphasised by the fact that it was they who decided to raise the price of *The Chronicle* (not then a year old) from fourpence to sixpence. The following year, the Old Girls spent the weekend nearest to Ascension Day at Queen Anne's, and this was the pattern for the next nine years. On the Saturday there was an afternoon river picnic, followed by Evening Chapel. After that, they all had supper in the Dining Hall, with speeches, and the evening ended with music and charades. On Sunday, they attended a Celebration of Holy Communion in Chapel, and later both Matins and Evensong, with a sermon at each. From old records it is clear how much they looked upon their attendance at School Chapel as the highlight of their weekend. Finally, on Sunday evening, they were entertained to supper by Miss Holmes and all her staff. In every way it was made clear that they were still an integral part of Queen Anne's. This close connection was emphasised by the suggestion that there should be a special Old Girls' hatband. It must be remembered that at that time boaters were fashionable, so the idea was less strange than it may seem now. The hatband was to be blue with red and white edges, and a white rose embroidered on the front. By 1901 these hatbands were available, and continued for the next seven years, when, no doubt because of changing fashions, they were replaced by a specially designed brooch. The older generation of today's Old Girls will know these brooches well.

Like all growing societies, the O.G.S. gradually had to accept more and more organisation. Three years after Miss Holmes' hopeful idea that no rules would be needed, the decision was taken that the rules of the Society were to be printed, and a copy given to each member. Among the requirements for membership at that time was one which must seem strange to the present day: each member was required to read three books from a published list before the date of the next meeting, each year. Some form of directed further education was clearly thought necessary, even if only in a very minor way, and some of these young women may well have left school at fifteen. The lists of books published give a wide choice—for instance, one year's list contained both *Cranford* and *Paradise Lost*, hardly of comparable length or difficulty—and there was obviously much enthusiasm for the scheme among the Committee. The ordinary members of the Society seem to have felt less zeal, as after one year the publication of a new list of books was accompanied by the warning that a fine of sixpence would be demanded from each Old Girl who had not read her books.

It must sometimes have been difficult for Miss Holmes to remember that her Old Girls were no longer within her jurisdiction, particularly in the early days. From its beginning in 1898, *The Chronicle* was designed to be the school magazine, with the word 'school' widely interpreted. Accounts of events, information on school charities, financial matters, academic success or victories on the games field, all were of interest equally to the school of the time and to the Old Girls. It is, therefore, easy to understand that, when a different format for *The Chronicle* was proposed after 10 years, the views of the Old Girls were considered important. What was obviously not very encouraging was the lack of actual financial support for *The Chronicle*; and it was pointed out that, though by then there were 183 members of the O.G.S., only 57 were subscribing their annual one shilling and sixpence for *The Chronicle*. This explains why before long an O.G.S. subscription was instituted, to include a copy of *The Chronicle* each year, with one shilling and sixpence from the subscription ear-marked annually for this purpose. This arrangement continued right into the 1960s, when it was sadly decided that the present school purchasers of *The Chronicle* could no longer subsidise the O.G.S. to the extent then needed, and there was a split into a *School Chronicle*, and an O.G.S. Newsletter. Fortunately, Miss Holmes and the early members of the Society had built well, for the idea that the school, past and present, is an entity was deeply rooted, and easily survived the financial problems which beset *The Chronicle*. Miss Holmes always gave a great welcome to her Old Girls, and that warmth of welcome has certainly persisted.

The statement made by Miss Holmes when the O.G.S. was founded indicates her own concern for others, and she expected her girls to share this concern. She recognised that they were in many ways privileged, and to her it was perfectly obvious that any form of privilege entailed responsibility, a need to do whatever was possible to improve the lives of the less fortunate. She believed in practical help. Until there was a School Chapel, the girls attended St Giles Church in Reading on Sundays, and it was in this parish that a need was found which they could help to answer. Some young girls going into domestic service for the first time came from families who were not able to provide them with all they needed. So working parties were set up at Queen Anne's and there the girls sewed clothes to be handed over to the parish for use by those who needed them to start out on their work. Maybe some people today would condemn this as patronising, but who is to say that such human approach to a problem is less desirable than faceless state bureaucracy? The help certainly reached those who needed it.

By the time the Chapel was built, Queen Anne's had joined the United Girls' Schools Mission, and much of the school's charitable interests became more organised. The Mission was based in London at Camberwell, and trouble was taken to see that the girls knew as much as possible about the work and could therefore develop a lively interest in it. One of the earliest appeals to them was for secondhand clothes, readable books, and, an interesting request, for flowers, all to be sent to Camberwell. During the first year, arrangements were made with the U.G.S.M. for two boys to come to Caversham and stay in the village for a convalescent holiday after they had been ill. This was obviously successful as the experiment was repeated another year. Here was the beginning of the sports and picnics for what would now be called deprived children, when the school acted as host. These special days managed to outlast two World Wars. There was nothing automatic or impersonal in the response of the girls to the U.G.S.M., and the annual service in London was always attended by a number of girls and several members of staff. Special speakers came down from the Mission at least once a year to arouse interest and gain support. On one occasion two girls went up to Camberwell to help with the special tea provided as a treat for the boys' school in which the Mission was interested. Every issue of *The Chronicle* during these years contained a detailed report on the work of the U.G.S.M., and, as part of the school, members of the Old Girls' Society gave much financial support. Inevitably, with the years, the needs changed and the personal enthusiasm waned, though certainly not in the time of Miss Holmes, or for many a year after her.

Those who think that sponsoring an African child in need of help is a comparatively modern development should consult the early history of Queen Anne's. From almost the very first years a child was adopted by the girls as a special kind of sister. Letters were sent to this child and some practical support given. It is clear from the records that the scheme was very successful, and that the girls took a great interest in their African 'sister'. Miss Holmes and her school showed in this as in so much else their belief that help should be given where it was needed, whether locally, nationally or internationally, and that such help should be as personal as possible.

No school exists in a vacuum and of course many important national events during these years had their effect on Queen Anne's. Started in the final part of Queen Victoria's reign, the school naturally marked the end of that era with a Memorial Service for her in Chapel. Annually, Empire Day was commemorated with the singing of the National Anthem, and in time the custom was established whereby every girl wore a daisy as a badge of the Empire. The Coronation of King George V on 21 June 1911 was the occasion for a special service in Chapel using one of the official forms of service provided. Two days later, all the girls went down into the village to see an early motion picture of the Coronation.

The Great War of 1914 to 1918 naturally made a considerable impact, and there was hardly any girl who did not have relatives or friends serving. Everyone felt involved. The school was trained to consider other people and to look out for those in need of help, so it would have been no surprise to anyone, that first Christmas of the war, to have found the usual party turned into a special Christmas Tree Party for the Belgians living at that time in Caversham. Throughout the war no away matches were played, and the money saved in this way was spent on cardigans and caps for British soldiers at the Front: the school particularly supported the 113th Battery of the Royal Field Artillery. Money was also set aside to provide comforts for the Belgian Army each Christmas. The Chapel was twice borrowed by the R.A.S.C., and the school enjoyed the pageantry of the soldiers marching accompanied by bagpipes and drums, a sight which certainly brought the war nearer. Some of the girls made sandbags and respirators to be sent to the troops abroad. The School Chaplain, the Rev. C. O. Jenkyn, known to all the girls as Jenks, left in 1915 to become the Army Chaplain, another strong personal link for the school with the progress of the war. It was a time of austerity in every way, recalled as being bleak and cold, but there seems to have been no coal shortage, for there was always a big, open fire in the gymnasium when it was used as a Hall. Newspaper cuttings were read there to the girls, while they got on with their mending or their knitting for the troops. Sacrifices during this time were expected, and indeed taken for granted: for instance, prize winners each year throughout the war were given their prizes as money, to be immediately handed back to buy comforts for those at the Front. Like everyone else at that time, the girls did what they could to help. Miss Holmes would never have tolerated a school which did anything less. It was sad for her that she was no longer at Queen Anne's to celebrate the Peace.

The factual history of these years shows the beginning and the development of ideas and events still to be found today, or only very recently discontinued: Mark Reading, for instance, is officially referred to by 1909, and the expression seems to have been in use well before that; and the name of Special Choral was used for the school choir by 1912, with its corollary that all the girls in the school formed the choir for Chapel singing, hence Saturday morning Choirs. The school building was always spoken of by Miss Holmes as a house; no doubt the quotation from Psalm 127 round the porch fitted with this, but mainly it seems it was because she intended it to be a house, a kind of home, rather any form of institution. This explains why the headmistress's room in school was known until very recently as the Drawing Room, and why for many years it housed a piano as well as normal drawing-room furniture; parents were received there are as they would have been as visitors in a home, and parties of many kinds took place there. The school Carol Service as a community act of worship at the end of Christmas term dates back to these early days, and the playing of handbells by the Sixth Form has been part of that service since before the First World War. Report cases and report forms remained the same for well over 70 years, until the need for ease of report writing by non-resident staff meant the gradual introduction of leaflet reports. Some events have a long history also. The first recorded visit to a Bradfield Greek play was in 1900, and it was about then that the long-standing tradition began by which the prefects or Sixth Form entertain the staff at the end of each summer term. Elderly people living in Caversham have been entertained from very early days and Special Choral and the School Orchestra made their contribution, just as they have done so many times since.

Perhaps the clearest example of the birth of tradition comes from the early celebrations of Ascension Day, which has always been kept as the school's birthday. Picnics for everyone started from the very beginning, and continued until the '60s when the area had become much more built-up and the safety of groups of girls roaming out in the country could no longer be guaranteed. To begin with, the girls used to drive to their destination in brakes, as for instance in 1899 when they travelled to the hills above Marlow—except for four or five very energetic girls who cycled there, and back. The places chosen for these picnics awaken echoes in the memories of many succeeding generations: Nettlebed, Christmas Common, Burnham Beeches, villages above the Thames, Checkendon Woods, all of them were used, and the river was always there and waiting. By 1908, coaches were beginning to be used, and that year the school went by train to Slough and then on to Burnham Beeches by coach. All went well on the way out, but on the return one coach broke down, and one can almost hear some comments on these new-fangled combustion engines. Two years later once again there were problems. The girls, as so often, took a train and then walked; but the dashing Chaplain, the Rev. C. Jenkyn, drove a car in which he took Miss Mason who ran one of the outside boarding houses. Alas for his attempt to be up-to-date and adventurous, for on the way he drove his car into a stream. He and his passenger arrived at the picnic decidedly late, and it seems a pity that no record survives of their reception. On Ascension Day evenings there were always special staff dinners, and starting from the very first of those birthday dinners the prefects provided small posies of flowers for each member of staff just as they have done ever since.

In many ways, therefore, the present-day Queen Anne's girl would certainly not be entirely at sea were she to be transported back over all the years, and many small details would seem to her exactly the same. Most of all, she might well feel at home in a community where generously interpreted Christian values mattered, just as they do today, and she might spare a thought for the Headmistress who imprinted them so firmly on her school. The Grey Coat Hospital had utilised the initials of its name to form its motto, 'Generous, Courteous and Honourable', and following on the same idea the motto chosen for Queen Anne's School was, 'Quietness and Strength'. Later generations may have smiled when seeing it carved in wood and fixed to the wall in a noisy gymnasium, but to Miss Holmes it was exactly what she wanted for her girls, and indeed what she herself exemplified. There was nothing showy or pretentious about her, and she showed the strength of her faith in everything she did. On the foundation stone of the School Chapel is to be found the quotation, 'Worship the Lord in the beauty of holiness', and the choice of this must surely have been inspired by her.

Just as in all the furnishing of that Chapel she looked for the very best and most beautiful available in her time, so too she knew how to surround herself with interesting and attractive objects to create an impression of the comforts of home. One of her past pupils, who knew her in her last year at Queen Anne's, speaks of her interesting Italian pictures, her easy chairs ready for her visitors of any age, and of the sense of warm comfort that emanated from the Drawing Room. She made that room a centre for the school, and it seemed both natural and fitting that the school's first grand piano, bought through the girls' own efforts, should be placed there. It may have been comparatively easy for her to know her early boarders very well, but she achieved the same kind of relationship with all the girls throughout her time at Caversham. To help towards this, every evening she shook each girl by the hand and wished her good-night. At the end of a term, those learning music (which then meant practically everyone) went to the Drawing Room to play to her to show what they had learnt. Every new girl had to go to her to play the piano—and ignorance of this skill was no excuse, she had to go just the same. No doubt Miss Holmes realised that the children were more at ease when some activity was required of them. She had the knack of finding small, imaginative presents for the young ones to reward them for any little successes. Her Old Girls had real affection for her, as was shown by their gift to her of the pony, Kitty, to draw her cart. In *The Chronicle* of 1911 she quoted, for girls of 20 years of age, A. E. Housman's poem 'Loveliest of trees, the cherry'; this was her way of encouraging them to use time well and to seek for beauty. Achievement was an additional pleasure, but what mattered was the kind of people the girls became. Her 1909 letter to her Day Girls deserves to be quoted as the epitome of what she wanted for all her pupils: they were to be 'public-spirited and courageous, simple-hearted and loyal, and, in fact, to try to be everything that is worth being, and so to help your School to be what its founders meant it to be'.

Tradition and a proper understanding of the past were important to her. She was obviously proud of the old Foundation, and determined that Queen Anne's should be a worthy part of it. She and Miss Day, the headmistress of the Grey Coat Hospital, were on good terms with each other, and the distance between the two schools proved to be no problem. She accepted graciously any help that was offered, while seeing to it that her own school learnt to help itself, by its own efforts raising money, for instance, to provide an East Window for Chapel, or an organ, or whatever it might be that was needed. Just as important to her were the needs of those outside the school who faced deprivation or distress of any kind. She taught her girls to offer personal help wherever possible, and also to look as widely as they could: it was typical of her that on her first visit to India she pinpointed the problems that would follow from too much British interference with the old traditional Indian gods and beliefs.

The last years Miss Holmes spent at Queen Anne's were overshadowed by the First World War, but she faced this with quiet courage, and urged her girls to do the same. Even before the war started she was commending to them the need to make 'a brave venture' towards a better world, and exhorting them not to be discouraged by any fears of the unknown. The 21st birthday of the school was in 1915, and in spite of the war it was made an occasion for celebration. It was then that the portrait of Miss Holmes, now in the School Hall, was given to the school. No one who looks at that portrait can help seeing that calm serenity which was her hall-mark, and it seems to interpret perfectly her favourite lines from Rabindranath Tagore: 'Only let me make my life simple and straight, like a flute of reed, for Thee to fill with music'. The portrait was presented, with a speech by Miss

Wordsworth, from Lady Margaret Hall, and she used five adverbs to describe the way the work done by Miss Holmes had progressed: 'gradually, gently, softly, lovingly and beneficially'. They cannot be bettered.

When she retired in 1917, her leave-taking of the school she had created was as quiet and calm as one would expect, for her work there was finished. She died in 1947, and two memorials to her were established: first, the two large wooden candlesticks in the Sanctuary of the School Chapel she loved; and second, the formation of the Holmes Memorial Fund to help girls at school who were in difficulties. Both were entirely fitting for this truly Christian lady. Her real and lasting memorial must be Queen Anne's itself.

Chapter III

The Second Headmistress
Miss Kathleen E. Moore, 1918-1939

The School's second headmistress was appointed towards the end of the First World War. During her 20 years' tenure Queen Anne's reputation, and the size of the school, continued to grow. An indication of her strong personality and her influence on the character of the School was shown in part of the speech given by the Chairman of the Foundation, Canon C. S. Woodward, when the new Hall was opened in 1930.

> Your Headmistress is a lady who does not know the meaning of 'impossible' and, thanks to her energy, faith and enthusiasm we have at last secured the Hall which we have so long desired.

When she came to the School, pupils were realising that, partly through the work of women during the First World War, most would lead very different lives from those who left Queen Anne's only five years earlier. It would not just be ambitious and clever girls who would gain qualifications, but all would be encouraged to think of careers and jobs. 'Living at home', the occupation given by many Old Girls in the *School Chronicle* is seen less and less often as the years go by.

Miss Moore's time spans the recovery after the First World War, the era when she and her fellow teachers would get the vote, when old ideas were being questioned and possibly cast aside, and she needed to steer a course between the old and new.

She writes her first letter in the *School Chronicle* of September 1918 reporting that the School was growing fast and was waiting for the boarding house in Derby Road to be completed.

Miss Moore considered that her happy childhood in a large family in an English vicarage influenced her life. That was where she learnt to appreciate family affection, unity and loyalty. She attended Baker Street and Wimbledon High Schools and then went to London University, gaining a degree in Modern Languages. However, despite her high academic qualifications, she could not obtain any teaching post in England, so went to a small school in Southern Ireland. She was engaged to teach French, but found she was expected to teach Botany as well. When she explained to the Headmistress that she knew no Botany, a delightful Irish voice commented: 'That does not matter, my dear, neither do the girls!' At the end of six months she went to a new girls' school to be opened at Sherborne in Dorset, complementing the existing boys' public school. She taught there for seven years becoming a House Mistress and then Second Mistress.

11. Miss Moore.

Arriving at Queen Anne's she found that prices had soared through inflation caused by the First World War and School fees had not been raised. Expenditure had been cut drastically 'until salutary austerity became hardship and economy in housekeeping was bordering on malnutrition'. She arrived in January 1918, and by February had got the Governors to agree to raise the fees to the maximum permitted by the Commissioners, and gradually embarked on a building programme.

When she arrived, there was only one lab, no Domestic Science Room, no craftsroom, and the girls were always having to be evicted from the Lower Reference library (now the Staff Room) so that staff could eat their meals. The Boarding Houses were 'transit camps' where pupils stayed for a term or two until there was room in School House. They were known by their postal addresses as Hillside, The Hill and Oakfield, and day girls were given postal addresses and called 'Amershams'. There was little contact outside form rooms between School House and the isolated communities in Boarding Houses. There were already in School seven games teams called after the seven Founders, which had Colours and drew the loyalty of girls. It was Miss Moore's brilliant idea to take these teams and gradually create the House system, linking them with Boarding Houses, a system in which equal and independent parts were closely knit into the community of the school. In doing so she rescued the neglected eighth Founder, Mr. Wilkins.

In the 1918 *Chronicle* Miss Moore writes of the rapid growth of the Boarding Houses, and plans to unite them closer to School House. Sitting rooms in School House for Out House girls were established, Miss Moore herself providing curtains, floor coverings and cushions. On Saturdays pupils were responsible for cleaning and polishing the sitts, where many had cushions embroidered in House Colours. It was also the custom to wear House Colours knitted in wool round the bottom of sweaters. The form gardens were dug up and apportioned as House gardens. Houses were now linked officially, being paired as follows: Boulte and Maddock, Holmes and Wilkins, Michell and Webbe, Wisdome and Ffyler, with each pair of houses containing about 60 girls, and day pupils were allotted to School Houses, the 'in' Houses.

In the same *Chronicle* girls at the school were asked to contribute original articles for the first time, the *Chronicle* previously having been a calendar of past events and a record of the Old Girls' Association meeting. But the names of pupils who had passed public examinations were omitted 'to economise on paper'.

The whole School went into Reading one day in 1918, to see King George V and Queen Mary, and because of the war there was no Ascension Day outing, just 'picnic walks'. Following a lecture on War Savings the School National Savings Association was started with a representative from each form collecting weekly subscriptions. Within six months the 198 members had saved £371 17s. 4d.

Many of the Old Girls were doing different kinds of War Work. Joyce S. Scott wrote in the *Chronicle* of some of her experiences in France as a Y.M.C.A. chauffeuse. The Old Girls' news reports on others who were doing war work from office jobs, working on the land, nursing or being V.A.Ds., while many married ex-pupils were now war widows. Another Old Girl writes: 'I worked in the Ministry of Munitions and, when the laboratory burnt down, had to be rescued by firemen from the high building with the roof alight and we were all suffering from the fumes of the chemicals'.

In November 1918 the School was part of the national influenza epidemic. Because of the number of cases it was closed on Armistice Day, 11 November, not reopening until the following week. This prompted a poem in the May 1919 *Chronicle* (see Appendix E).

Pupils had been asked to write a new school song instead of 'Follow Up'—but as one contributor wrote in the *Chronicle* 'what rhymes with Queen or Anne or Caversham or Quietness and Strength?' However, Juliet Crawley-Boevey used 'length' with Quietness and Strength when she wrote the school vesper which was in use by 1935 and is still sung today (see Appendix F); indeed it will be during the Centenary Service in Westminster Abbey in 1994.

The first Speech Day for several years was held in 1919 when Miss Moore commented: 'A great deal will fall on girls and now they have great opportunities'. She also mentioned that there were no cups for swimming. Two were donated the following year and presented for the first time in 1920. The first Singing Competition was held in the December and won by Holmes.

To celebrate the school's 25th birthday a river picnic was held on 29 May 1919. The steamer, *Majestic*, was hired and sailed up river to Goring where everyone disembarked for tea in a field. On returning to school pupils and staff found that the Old Girls had decorated the dining room patriotically in red, white and blue and a small buttonhole of flowers was laid by each plate.

The following year a similar Ascension Day Outing was planned, but pupils volunteered to forego the excursion, and £25 was given to the Save the Children Fund because of the urgent appeal on behalf of the starving children in Austria and Central Europe as a result of the War. Instead pupils had a picnic in Dyson's Wood, and the girls also knitted and made garments which were sent to Austrian children.

The first time that a charabanc outing is mentioned is 1921 when pupils were taken by coach to Bucklebury Common, except for prefects and some staff who cycled there. A photograph of the time shows the line of parked open top single deck coaches, and the bobbing white hats of the girls seated in rows. In 1922 the steamer *Majestic* was again chartered with *River Queen*, and the Ascension Day trip was to Goring with lunch on board. Then the energetic ones climbed Streatley Hill.

In 1925 on Ascension Day the school had lunch on a steamer whilst sailing to Greenlands, beyond Henley, where there were two hours ashore to tour the house (and grounds) belonging to Viscount Hambleden.

The following year it seemed that the Ascension Day picnic by steamer would have to be postponed because of the General Strike, but when that was called off on 12 May the School had its usual birthday picnic the next day.

Leisure time at the School was strictly supervised and many pupils did not leave the premises at all during term time. However, this should be seen in conjunction with the background of the era when young girls were chaperoned when not at home, and few expected to be entertained or given the opportunities that exist today.

In 1923 the activities at Autumn Half Term for those remaining in School included matches between Long Hair and Bobbed Hair—teams with the modern short hairstyles winning. Other girls played on the Giant Strides in the Gym, an apparatus of rope ladders and bars hung from the ceiling which swung round with the momentum of the gymnasts, and the rest occupied themselves with mending! The weekend was too wet for a Firework Display so these were let off the following Saturday on Armistice Day.

Girls were only allowed to leave the school premises with suitable escorts twice a term, written permission having to be sought first. Sunday walks were in crocodiles supervised by mistresses, while only senior girls were ever allowed to walk to the shops at Reading in small groups a couple of times a term. So with such a restricted regime the half-term entertainments, Saturday evening lectures, and Christmas party were eagerly anticipated.

Reporting on the calendar of events in 1922 S.C. James of the Sixth writes that

> The subjects of the lectures were British Wild Animals and How to Tame Them. The Sudan lecture was originally intended to be on Egypt, but owing to an accident to the slides the lecturer changed his subject to the Nile and there were good lantern slides of the Country and its peculiar inhabitants.

The following year the Governors presented the school with its own lantern for illustrated lectures, which may have prevented further accidents to the slides and added to S. C. James' knowledge of North Africa!

A new Debating Society was formed by the Literary Society in 1922 and was to have fluctuating fortunes over the years—sometimes being well supported and other years not holding any debates. The first motion was 'that capital punishment should be abolished' and this was carried. A lecture was given by a speaker from the League of Nations. He explained the aims of the League to keep the peace and its declaration 'that no nation may declare war without first giving nine months' warning of its intentions'. However, he mentioned that some countries such as Germany, Russia and America had not yet joined. It was hoped to start a Junior League at Queen Anne's. The Scientific Society could not go on a visit to Huntley and Palmer's Biscuit Factory in Reading because of a scarlet fever epidemic in Reading.

Later that year a number of senior pupils went to the U.G.S.M. commemorative service in Southwark Cathedral, and were shown over the settlement hostel and children's rooms. This first visit was the start of many as the link between Q.A.S. and the Peckham Settlement grew. Also for the first time senior pupils visited the settlement of the United Girls' Schools Mission in London, and gave a party for 60 children up to 10 years of age, while others made clothes.

The Scientific Society was given an electric lantern in 1926, and so three lectures with slides were given. 'It is much easier to manage than the oxy-hydrogen one', was the comment, and presumably far safer and more reliable. Among papers read was one on 'Wireless' and there were visits to Huntley and Palmer's factory and Reading Ice and Cold Storage Factory.

Until 1921 the Head Girl of QAS had always edited the *Chronicle*, but in September 1922 it was decided to form a committee and a member of staff would be editor.

12.   Cricket.

The number of Old Girls belonging to the Association was growing, and in the early 1920s they formed into 11 groups in different parts of England. In 1921 it was agreed that if an Old Girl had not paid her subscription for three years she would cease to belong to the Association. However, to shame them the names of those in arrears were read out at the meeting. Life membership at that time was 10 shillings (50 pence) which included the annual *Chronicle*.

In September 1922 it was reported that seven ex-pupils were at Oxford University, three at Cambridge, ten at London and two at Edinburgh. A further nine were taking teacher training, another domestic science training, four girls were on secretarial courses and five doing Physical Training, 'while others are doing useful work at home'.

A party went to the Greek Play at Bradfield which was revived for the first time since the First World War, and girls were impressed by the Greek Theatre, the grandeur of the chorus and the accompaniment of flutes and lyres.

The tradition of excellence at lacrosse was well established and matches are reported such as those in 1918 when the QAS team beat Godstowe by 21 goals to nil and the Savoyards second beat Reading College Ladies by a crushing 28 goals to nil.

It must have been a wet summer in 1922. The away cricket match against Wycombe Abbey could not be finished. Rain fell throughout the match against Downe House at home, but play continued with QAS making 125 for nine declared. Downe House were 12 for nine when their games mistress said the match must end as the team had to leave! Once again it was a successful year for the lacrosse team who won 10 of the 11 fixtures.

In 1926 the first lacrosse team won all its 15 outside matches. There were now five Old Girls in the England team, one in the Scottish and three were reserves for England.

When Miss Moore first arrived only cricket and swimming took place in the summer as there were no tennis courts. This was to change in 1921 when a fund was started to raise £1,000 to buy the archery field, which was land adjoining the playing field, and pupils organised a fête in the summer which raised £70. Money was still being collected for the Playing Field Fund in 1922 and a Midsummer Fair raised £500. Pupils thought of many novel ways of fund raising; the Fourth Form cleaned bicycles and kettles, the Prefects' Make and Mend Society sewed blouses and camisoles and darned stockings, whilst other pupils made Christmas gifts and baked cakes for birthday parties. Still more money was raised through performances of the School play, *The School for Scandal*, at the Balmore Hall, Reading. This was the first well coached and stage managed play by pupils for some years and a high standard of acting was reached.

In 1924 a new cloakroom and accommodation for changing after games were opened for day girls as well as two new classrooms and a small lab for advanced science. During the Autumn Term two classes worked in the swimming pool because of the noise and inconvenience from the work above their rooms. The old unheated swimming pool, a narrow building, was situated at the bottom of the Quad. When the 'swimmer' was being used for lessons a tarpaulin was suspended in the middle to divide the two classes. Reading Gas Company produced radiators to heat the area and Newman, the school's long-time caretaker, made steps so that staff and pupils could reach the desks and blackboards in the bottom of the swimming bath. The outer wall on the Quadside of this building was used for 'banging'—practising with a tennis racquet and ball by lines of aspiring Wimbledon entrants.

13.   The Hill.

Drawing and handwork classes were held in the Sanatorium (which was a building on the far side of the Henley Road) as the studio was not available. When the work was completed it was found that the new Small Lab lived up to its name, being so tiny that girls had to be meticulous at tidying up and putting apparatus away. Despite this in 1926 the first Science Scholarship was won by a QAS girl and Mary Gray (Mrs. McDonald) went to Girton.

The lease at the Hill in Surley Row, now the home of the local member of parliament, Sir Anthony Durant, ran out. A new house which was to become Ffyler would be built at the top of the field, but in the meantime Avenue House in Woodcote Road was rented. This was a long way from the main buildings and girls were driven back to this boarding house in relays in the evenings, 'but in the morning they will enjoy the walk', Miss Moore said firmly in her Speech Day report.

By 1926 the new house (Ffyler) was completed and connected to Eastfield, then Wilkins and now Maddock, with the same kitchens serving both. Girls were delighted with

14. Ffyler.

15.   Staff of 1926. In the front row are: Miss Faull (1st left), Miss Weeden (2nd left), Miss Osyth Potts (4th left), Miss Coleman (6th left) and Miss Mc Nish (3rd right). In the middle row are: Miss Gascoigne (5th left), Miss Edwards (6th left) and Miss Sailman (7th left).

the dormitories furnished with coloured curtains and matching tiled washstands. Even during Miss Scott's time girls were reluctant to allow these washstands to be replaced by more modern, but less sturdy furniture.

When Speech Day came round in June 1926, the Governors decided to give a prize to every girl passing Higher or School Certificate of the Oxford and Cambridge Joint Boards, or Final or Advanced Grades of Music Examinations of the Associated Board.

The first report of a school trip abroad is in 1926 when twelve girls, three teachers, an Old Girl and Nurse were guided round Paris by Madame Maurel. 'No one bothers to observe the rules of the road, so we got a gendarme to hold up the traffic for all eighteen of us to cross safely', writes a pupil describing the week's visit.

Earlier a Government Inspector had stated that he was satisfied with the School and its progress, but thought there should be an assembly room large enough to hold all the pupils, and this was also stressed by the Duchess of Atholl, one of the first women Members of Parliament, at Speech Day. She was Parliamentary Secretary to the Board of Education, and a fellow school pupil of Miss Moore. Addressing the School and parents on Speech Day, the Duchess said that more girls were staying at school longer and going on to university or teacher training and she hoped many would go into professional life.

'Women have responsibilities I did not dream of when I left school, such as the vote'.

In 1926 there were 42 School Certificates awarded with 13 Matriculations (a higher standard) from 44 candidates.

In the Sergeants' Drill Competition the Section led by Margaret Catley (Mrs. Ainger) obtained 93 marks out of a hundred, beating the other nine sections and winning the cup. An inter-house gymnastic competition was also held for the first time.

In September before school re-assembled 92 Old Girls came for their reunion weekend. At the 1927 Speech Day Miss Moore emphasised the difficulties without a hall.

When examinations are held the gym goes, no singing classes can be held for 14 days, and we can hold no entertainments indoors to which visitors can be invited. When it is wet we use the house sitting rooms but they are over the gym and useless for anything noisy. You must appreciate the difficulties of keeping a hundred and eighteen girls quiet for a fortnight, especially if it is wet.

She reported that the cost of building Ffyler was being repaid to the Foundation by instalments so the Governors were unable to find money to build a hall. 'Eight old gentlemen in Westminster each gave five shillings in 1689—a much larger sum than the £10 being asked of all parents', she said in her appeal. Planning went ahead and £900 was raised during a fête in 1928. The Foundation Stone was laid on Speech Day 1929 by Bishop Shaw when a service was held in the Quad and the school presented *Antigone* on the front lawn.

During that year and the following the building of the new hall continued. In 1930 H.R.H. Princess Mary, Countess of Harewood (the daughter of King George V) visited QAS on 21 June to open it. A commemorative programme gives details of the Royal Visit including the concert by the School in the Hall before the Princess arrived.

16.   Opening of the Hall by Princess Mary.

She was received by Her Grace the Duchess of Atholl, Canon Barry of Westminster, Canon C. S. Woodward (chairman of the Foundation), and the headmistress, Miss Moore. Other dignitaries were presented to her in the Drawing Room, the Headmistress' room. At the door of the Hall the architect was presented to her and as she entered the School Orchestra played the National Anthem.

As well as declaring the Hall officially open Princess Mary presented the awards and prizes. The Hall was packed with some seven hundred parents, staff and pupils and many others who could not get in took it in turns to peer through the windows at the celebrations. Princess Mary was presented with a bouquet and a Prefect's Badge, which at that time was made of gold.

Miss Moore listed some of the many gifts to the Hall including a carved Cromwellian chair in which Princess Mary sat and four similar chairs made from old beams of St John's College, Oxford; an antique refectory table, a clock, her own portrait, oak steps, and the chairs which were gifts of past and present girls and were all named on the backs.

That year the new house for Maddock, now Wilkins, next to the School, was opened, and this and its garden were much appreciated. A homecraft course at Hillside was started for girls in their last year, and the County tennis courts at the end of the field were acquired for the School.

By now the bulk of the Reference Library had been transferred to the new library above the Hall. Miss Moore gave two large tables for this library, and girls enjoyed working in its calm atmosphere and using the window seats on the whole length of one side.

The Old Girls belonging to the London Group raised £50 and this provided curtains for the new stage in the Hall. These were used to effect in February 1931 when *The Admirable Crichton* was staged. The sale of tickets at 1s. 6d. (approximately seven pence each) raised £50 and £40 was given to the UGS Settlement Fund to buy the building in Stafford Street, London. Some pupils went to London and presented the money to Queen Mary when she opened the new Settlement House.

The new Hall was used for many events, and plays could be performed with a proper stage. Ffyler produced *Little Women*, Wilkins *Leatherface* (noted in the House Book as an unhistorical incident in 1572) and the

17.   The fiction library.

Prefects staged *Grand Opera Gloria*! Programmes and posters for these plays and many others are in the School Archives.

The workmen who had built the Hall were given a supper by the Governors and Miss Moore when the Sixth Form put on an entertainment. They then asked for a holiday for the School which was granted for the following March. Everyone enjoyed the Christmas party even more than usual, because there was so much room for games and dancing.

An Inter-Schools Music Festival was held at QAS in 1932 because of the facilities of the new Hall.

To mark 21 years at QAS the Chaplain, the Rev. C. O. Jenkyn and Mrs. Jenkyn, were given a book of school photographs and sketches presented and arranged by Old Girls. The following Easter he died suddenly whilst at a service in a local church.

Miss Moore wrote an appreciation of Cyril Jenkyn, saying that, when he came to Caversham, he was offered the post of Chaplain and came on trial for a month but stayed 21 years. During the First World War he left to become an Army Padre in France and was awarded the M.C. in 1916.

There was an old quince tree in the garden at Hillside. One year during the war it produced 1,000 pounds of fruit which was made into jam. But the weight pulled the tree sideways and the roots came out of the ground. It was to have been cut down. But while he was on leave Mr. Jenkyn, a keen bellringer, borrowed bell ropes and with the assistance of a team of girls hauled the old tree upright and it continued to flourish for many years.

In 1933 he taught a group of girls to ring handbells and they gave a short recital before and after the Carol Service. This tradition continued at the Carol Service for many more years.

A scheme to enlarge the Chapel and provide room for 80 more girls was put forward. Miss Moore wrote in the *Chronicle* that £800 would be needed for this but £500 was already in hand. In 1934 it was reported that the extension to the Chapel in memory of the Rev. Cyril Jenkyn would cost £2,000, and this was to be raised as £1,000 from the School and £1,000 from the Old Girls and friends. The Staff organised a sale of Christmas presents and raised £100. Other fund raising activities included a Nativity Play and a fête at summer half term. A calendar for 1935 was sold at two shillings (ten pence), and for every day there was a quotation given by Governors, Staff and girls. By Speech Day the overdraft had been reduced to £300 and by September was only £56 thanks to the generosity of the Guild of Berks, Bucks and Oxon Bellringers who donated £96 in memory of Cyril Jenkyn. The new aisle of the Chapel was dedicated by the Bishop of Buckingham, on 4 February 1934, and Mrs. Jenkyn gave a memorial tablet for her husband which was placed on the chapel wall.

In 1935 a new window in the Chapel was dedicated to a Wisdome pupil, Lillias Palairet, who died suddenly one holiday. This represented the Guardian Angel with a spreading rainbow of coloured wings covering two QAS girls wearing their red cloaks; one holding the lily of purity and the other the olive branch of peace.

An Old Girl, Marian Gobius, sculpted an athletic figure for the Dutch section of the Art Exhibition attached to the Olympic Games being staged in Los Angeles. It was the statue of a girl in QAS games uniform. She has a 'Good Position' on her gym badge and a 1st

18. 'Trics'. Back row, left to right: Helen Gould, Joan Parry, Rosamund Bond, Hilary Green, D. Fearon(?), Margaret Horne, Mary Utterton, Helen Rowntree; front row: Marjorie Higgs, Betty Evans, Eleanor Crichton-Miller, Mary Edwards.

XII brooch on her House tie. With ruffled hair in a 1930s bob she leans on her lacrosse stick and was titled 'Half Time'. Unfortunately the school was not able to afford a bronze replica of the statue, but Marian modelled a small figure and this was presented to the School to be used as a 'Crosse' (now goal) trophy, and still is an unique award.

A 1934 photograph of the 1st Lacrosse team shows the girls in their pleated red 'gymmers', all buttoned up to the neck with collars and ties, and cinched with a webbing belt that had leather straps and buckles. Originally this was some three inches wide and very unflattering to all but the slimmest. Later the width of the belt was reduced by half.

The long sleeves of the games tunic ended in a buttoned cuff and were decorated with the 'Sergeants' stripes of those who were Section Leaders in the drill held at Break in the Quad. The team members also wore red woollen knickers as well as long red stockings and were expected to finish matches just as immaculately dressed. The basic tie was a plain darkish blue, but House ties were worn for House matches and first teams had special ties of green and red stripes.

Old Girl, 'Cesca Blyth (Mrs. Sharpe), recalls that on a day with a gym class pupils wore a square-necked short-sleeved red sweater over the 'gymmer' which was removed before the lesson to create the outfit known as 'fuggers and bags'.

Later the tunics were referred to as 'trics', and the belts were elastic. A surviving prospectus of the 1930s gives the Clothes List and states that no necklaces, bangles or rings are to be allowed at school, nor were patterned or voile dresses. If silk dresses were not washable they were to be in navy blue. One white silk shirt was essential and any dresses made by a dressmaker had to be of the School material purchased from Peter Jones in London.

The Clothes List included: a navy coat and skirt, one or two tussore silk dresses (long sleeves) with knickers to match, four woollen combinations or four vests, six to eight pairs of brown silkestia stockings (Peter Jones), three camisoles (if worn), three liberty bodices (if worn). These two items were later replaced by three bust bodices—to which cheeky young brothers were apt to ask 'why do they have to be bust?', now known as 'bras'. Two navy knickers and four drawers or linings, two dozen handkerchiefs, one mackintosh, hat and umbrella.

The Games outfit of ties, tunics, jersey and knickers, elastic belt with S-clasp, red stockings, field shoes and gym shoes, was to be purchased at school. For the summer term girls required 'one dark blue stockinette bathing dress and one helmet bathing cap!'

Girls were also expected to bring to school a well-equipped work-basket, a rug, a prayer book, a Revised Version Bible, and a 'bug-scraper' comb. 'Nit examination' continued for many years with a visiting inspector combing each girl in case of infestation.

At that time fees were £120 per annum, with the usual supplements for music, extra washing, etc.

The School hat was hated by the girls and there had been discussion in the '20s about replacing it with a more modern style. The white straw hats with their deep crowns worn all the year were given up at the end of the decade, and a black velour hat with the school badge worn instead. By the '30s the black velour had given way to a navy blue felt with a school ribbon trim round the crown. At one time all the hats for School House girls were kept in two cupboards near the door to the Quad. Pupils took any hat and hoped it fitted. These hats, a very expensive part of the uniform, were also disliked and had to be worn at all times outside the school—on outings or walks and also for Early Service in the Chapel. Leavers would celebrate by tossing their headgear out of the train going to Paddington or the tidier ones would thrust them into rubbish bins on the station.

In 1933 the wives of Indian traders who were delegates to a Round Table Conference were entertained at the school and then presented a clock. This was hung in the front hall as the school's official timepiece and known to generations of girls as 'Begums'.

During the summer holidays of 1934 the school was fully connected to electricity and central heating was also installed. Previously some parts of the school and corridors were lit by gas. Sometimes in winter girls had to break the ice on the water pitchers before washing in the morning. All dormitories had to have windows open at night unless there was a hailstorm. The cold water from each girl's ewer was added to the small puddle of hot water poured into the bowls by maids at 7.00 a.m. However, there was no electricity in the old San building in Henley Road. This was then turned into a gaslit Domestic Science Room, and even in the 1940s girls learnt to iron with old fashioned flat irons heated on a stove. With electricity special flood lighting could be put into the Sanctuary of the extended Chapel. Also a new silver chalice was given by the Governors as the old one was not large enough for the bigger congregation.

In Spring Term 1934 the first lecture on 'Careers for Girls' is recorded and this was so popular that a further one was held later in the term.

For the lectures on Saturday evenings the girls wore their tussore silk frocks with white cardigans. School House supper was shredded wheat with oranges so that the cooks and maids could have the evening off.

Since the Hall could not be blacked out in the summer and it was too light to have lantern slides the girls enjoyed ballroom dancing—with each other. This was also the highlight after the supper at the 'Bust Up' when heads of Houses and forms would be expected to ask the mistresses to dance with them. Taller girls usually danced 'man' in the formal ballroom dances of the day performing athletic tangos, whirling round giddily in Viennese waltzes or mastering intricate steps in foxtrots and quicksteps. Frequent Paul Joneses meant that everyone had a chance to dance.

An innovation in 1935 was the Governors' plan to install shower baths to be used after every gym session and these were built in an old store room which, with a new floor, became a changing room with six warm showers.

The freehold of the tennis courts at the top of the Field was obtained and further building plans included enlarging and improving the Sanatorium.

The School Orchestra had improved over the years and a string class was started with 20 girls learning the violin, viola and cello, and from this the nucleus of a Junior Orchestra was formed.

As an experiment, in addition to the Old Girls' Weekend in September 1935 ex-pupils returned to the School for a day in July so that they could meet members of Staff and present pupils.

Instead of enlarging the old Sanatorium it had been decided to build a new one (now the Junior House) and the building work commenced. In 1938 Miss Moore completed the organisation of School House and new Sanatorium was opened—in time for an epidemic of German measles in the Spring Term.

In the summer a party of girls joined those from 14 other public schools and 15 girls' clubs for a summer camp run on the lines of the Duke of York's (later King George VI) camps for boys from mixed backgrounds.

At Speech Day Miss Moore said that the School was doing well academically with a State Scholarship and many ex-pupils gaining degrees.

She announced that she would be handing over to her successor, Miss Joan Elliot, at Christmas 1938. When she left Miss Moore gave the school a radiogram which for many years was used in the Hall.

The Bishop of Bristol (past Chairman of the Greycoat Foundation, Dr. C. S. Woodward), paid tribute to Miss Moore's 21 years as headmistress.

> She has succeeded in keeping in an ageing body a young, vigorous and live spirit. Miss Moore has in a unique sense been the driving force of the School and its inspiration. I have never known anyone quite so indomitable.

19.   The Sanatorium.

Another tribute was paid by Canon Barry of Westminster, Chairman of the Foundation, who said that Miss Moore had raised the School to a level on which it could hold its own with any girls' public school in England. Her real achievements were to be found in the lives and outlook of those she had trained, and it was in the gratitude and trust of those who had passed through the School and of their successors that her reward was to be found.

One of her pupils, 'Cesca Blyth (Mrs. Sharpe), remembers Miss Moore as a kind, compassionate and caring woman, who really knew and understood the raw material she was dealing with—some of this was very raw indeed. She also recalls her pride when she was made a School Prefect.

Three lasting memorials to Miss Moore remain—the addition to the field, the Hall and its library and the extension to the Chapel.

Miss Moore died in an Oxford Nursing Home on 29 April 1969 aged 94. She had visited the School often in her retirement, and as a permanent memorial the new Junior House was renamed the Moore House and a new recreation room was built on to it.

Chapter IV

The Third Headmistress
Miss Joan Elliot, 1939-1957

'From the first moment I saw the school I knew I would be happy here, and Miss Moore has passed on her enthusiasm to me', was how Queen Anne's third headmistress introduced herself in the *Chronicle* of September 1939.

After a decade of new buildings and change of use of existing buildings the only new ones in 1939 were the Air Raid Shelters built on the field. Air Raid practices were carried out as regularly as Fire Drill.

War was declared on 3 September 1939 and, writing in the *Chronicle* at the end of that month, Miss Elliot said that the School had already accepted an Austrian refugee, and other nationalities including a Danish girl and an Indian girl. At the July 1939 Speech Day she had referred to the 1938 Munich crisis and said she hoped 'next year would find the world less anxious than at present'.

20.   Miss Moore, Miss Elliot, Canon Woodward and other members of the governing body.

She was frustrated that the Governors had been obliged to stop spending money on sensible things and instead had to excavate the field (near where the new Muriel Hall library now stands) for the Air Raid shelters. 'However, I hope they will give some guarantee of peace of mind and sense of security at any future time to parents.' She said that QAS had shared the restlessness of the country. However, it had been decided not to evacuate the school to a safer area, but to build the shelters instead.

Staff joined the Red Cross and practised driving at night without lights whilst wearing gas masks. There had been two courses of Red Cross lectures in 1938 with 16 staff and 19 girls gaining Air Raid Precautions (full) certificates, and 12 staff and 23 girls had passed their First Aid Exam.

Bicycles were once more allowed for the Sixth Form. Girls were envious of pupils who had those with three speed gears rather than the old fashioned 'sit up and beg' type, some of which, inherited from older sisters, still had 'skirt guards' on the back wheels to prevent long skirts getting caught up or dirty on the spokes. Cyclists were allowed out in groups of four on Saturdays and could take tea with them.

The following year, 1940, the *Chronicle* did not appear until October. 'It has been a strange and distressing year', comments Miss Elliot.

Putney High School was evacuated to QAS at this time. QAS numbers dropped to about two hundred. Some girls who were abroad when war was declared were unable to return to England, others had been sent to North America for safety while some remained at home, especially those in more rural areas in the west and south-west.

At the beginning of the War with the drop in numbers Webbe became a day girl House. Later girls were to join the School from Wycombe Abbey when their buildings were taken over by the American Forces.

In the winters of 1939 to 1945 evening prep. was interrupted for five minutes at varying times for 'black-out'. Every member of staff and all pupils shared in this duty with a staff patrol going round the school twice nightly warning of carelessly drawn blinds or curtains and quenching any accidental glimmer of light.

Walking up the field in the evening was dark and hazardous, so it was decided that Boarding House girls should not have to return to School House in the evenings.

Miss Elliot wrote later in the War:

> ... the black-out is not entirely a bad thing because now we can see the stars more clearly and so look outward and upward. We have been much blessed during these years of war and perhaps grown in intimacy and fellowship through the sharing of new duties and meeting of difficulties'.

Wartime regulations also forbade the ringing of the School or Chapel bells—church bells were only to be rung as a warning when the Country was invaded. For a short while in 1942 metal structures like wigwams were put on the field to stop invasion planes or parachutists landing.

With the shortage of petrol and 'erratic' railways there were few visitors to the school. Government posters everywhere asked 'Is Your Journey Really Necessary?' so both Speech Day and Old Girls' Day were cancelled.

A Sale of Work was held in November 1940 to raise money for War charities, and pupils made large numbers of 'comforts' for the troops by knitting socks, gloves and scarves. Michell's House Book records that 11 sweaters were knitted for shipwrecked Merchant Navy sailors in 1943.

To save paper the *Chronicle* had far fewer pages and original contributions were omitted.

However, the *Old Girls' News* reflected the position of the country. Many were in the various women's services, working in hospitals, or doing voluntary war work as well as a regular peace time job. Others had been evacuated with their families. Occupations listed included being a teacher evacuated with her school to near Whipsnade and having to walk two miles to the new school daily, another was working for the Czech Refugee Trust Fund; some did Womens' Voluntary Service work, another was a billeting officer, yet another job was cleaning rifles for the local Home Guard, and others were members of a Darning Depot looking after servicemen's socks!

One Old Girl writes of being evacuated to the country and taking Nanny to look after the children, but her domestics and gardener left to do war work, and she was busy driving round the locality in her car collecting household refuse for pig swill.

The Old Girls news included the tragic death on Active Service of Joan Campbell Forsyth in April 1941. She was an ambulance driver working in London during the Blitz. One night after being called out with a stretcher party she was returning home when the car took a direct hit and she and two others were killed outright. She had been a pupil from 1927 to 1933.

By October 1941 badges given included 'helpfulness in housework' and Gardening Colours were awarded. The staff continued to wash up after Sunday lunch at School House.

A company of Girl Guides was started for juniors and many of the seniors were still involved with the Red Cross. The over-fifteens were in the Girls Training Corps and later a Mechanised Transport Cadet Corps was formed and on Wednesday afternoons Army sergeants came to instruct and drill the girls. The uniform was of dark brown dungarees with the field belt worn with red gym blouses, walking shoes and a forage cap. Nearly all pupils over 15 joined the Girls' Training Corps and marched with other Women's Services through Reading in a parade during Warship Week and in other similar parades during the war years.

Every Wednesday all games and practices were cancelled as Wednesday became War Work Day. This was when the G.T.C. met, while younger girls belonged to the Junior Red Cross and the youngest to the Girl Guides. There were more than 70 Guides and 22 of them went to the Summer Camp.

Numbers of pupils increased and the buildings were still shared with Putney High School. They had afternoon lessons in the classrooms while Queen Anne's pupils were at Field. With the co-operation of Putney High School a Sale of Work was held for War charities and £350 was raised. Each House had stalls in a Form room and parents were asked to donate unrationed food for the School to sell. A buffet lunch was provided and the dining room was used for various side shows. Because of petrol rationing it was difficult to arrange away games matches and so there was only a small list of fixtures.

However, hockey was started and a match played against Putney High School, although it had to be cut short when the air raid siren sounded.

The School housed the priceless items belonging to the Grey Coat Foundation which were likely to be destroyed if they remained in London. These included the ancient charter granted by Queen Anne, portraits of the Founders (which were hung in the dining room), furniture and a strong box. This chest was made in 1710 and had an elaborate locking mechanism housed in the lid. The master key was able to unlock all its 12 locks at once. In it was placed an impress of the Charter Seal.

A smaller Speech Day was held in summer 1941 when Miss Elliot remarked that 'a scientific and classical learning was a constant thing in a changing world'. She reported that the food question had been helped by the vegetable garden where pupils worked. 'About clothes I need say little. Our visible lack of uniformity will be even more marked next year. Girls have knitted for the Forces and sewn garments for those in bombed areas and have been collected by lorry to help on local farms.' A Speech Day pageant of 'Girls through the Ages' included dancing, gym, singing and miming and the School Orchestra played. Miss Elliot planned and produced this.

Reading did not suffer from the early bombing raids of the Blitz when London and many other cities were bombed. However, on 11 December 1942, the Dramatic Society was performing a play for the Maids' Party, but it was interrupted when the warning siren went and everyone had to go to the shelters.

Girls had to be prepared to go to the Shelters at any time for several years. At night they left clothes ready to put on quickly and all had electric torches. After a while they did not have to go to the Shelters every time there was an air raid siren but were warned to be ready and only to leave the School buildings when the buzzer sounded.

In February 1943 the Germans bombed Reading during the day and the warning siren went. Sheila Hogarth (Mrs. Victor Jones) wrote to her parents:

> We were all having tea, although I was out in the passage by the dining room, when suddenly the whole place shook like a jelly and we heard a plane diving terribly low.
> As we went to the Shelters I looked up and saw a plane with black crosses, and then it machine gunned the School and the bullets went by the Chapel on the grass. There were girls coming over the field to School from Outhouses and they lay down and the German plane dived back over the School again, machine gunning as it went.

She wrote that no one at QAS was hurt but 'there were a great many casualties in Reading. Five bombs fell in Broad Street and shops and the Town Hall have been damaged and the 'Peoples' Pantry—that British Restaurant place—was completely demolished and St Lawrence's Church.'

All pupils had been issued with gas masks at the beginning of the War and everyone had to have hers with her at all times in case of a gas attack. Practices were held with everyone struggling into the masks as fast as possible. Early in the war a special van which could be pumped full of gas (probably tear gas rather than lethal mustard gas!) was parked outside School and all girls had to file through to test their masks.

In January 1944 Sheila wrote: 'We had two sirens last night and in the second one there was gun fire so at the unearthly hour of 4.45 a.m. we were traipsing round the orchard to the Shelters. I was jolly glad I'd got my siren suit'. (This was an all-in-one garment with trousers and usually a zip front so that it was quick to don.)

With restricted supplies and clothing being rationed the uniform had to be adapted. For field and gym the girls wore grey shorts and red blouses with red socks or stockings, while the few red tunic tricolenes were hoarded. The fortunate were the envied possessors of warm red cloaks, which had been passed on second or third hand through families and friends. The Sunday blue tussore frocks continued, but summer cotton frocks could be any pattern with short sleeves as long as they blue and white. For morning school girls wore navy skirts and natural Fair Isle jumpers with various designs on the collars and borders. In the evenings coloured wool frocks were permitted, but juniors had to wear blue science overalls to protect them from ink stains.

21. Old Girls' daughters, 1952.
Back row (*left to right*): S. Slade (*M. Horwood*), J. Govan (*M. Butler*), P. Broadhurst (*M. Griffiths*), A. Rowse (*E. Holmes*), R. Robertson (*M. Jewson*), P. Blair (*R. Allen*), A. McDonald (*M. Gray*), J. Warner (*W. James*).
Centre row: J. Gill (*M. Bishop*), R. Poutney (*B. Patch*), S. Powell (*M. Watkins*), S. Cave (*E. Paddick*), S. Dent (*H. Rowntree*), J. Stilwell (*F. Gauntlett*), M. McMullen (*C. Campbell*), S. Berthoud (*J. Waller*), A. Renison (*E. Gibb*).
Front row: A. Strafford (*G. Meyrick*), R. McMullen (*C. Campbell*), J. Lydall (*H. Woolston*), A. Wright (*B. Robinson*), W. Leonard (*B. Henman*), J. Albery (*M. Isaac*), G. Dickinson (*D. Utterton*), J. Robertson (*M. Jewson*), D. Ingram (*H. Williams*).

For walks there were navy blue costumes but no longer was the straw boater hat required in summer. Pupils wore navy felt hats or berets. Black shoes and stockings were changed to brown shoes and stockings. 'War time restrictions make it impossible for some girls to get recognised clothing', wrote Miss Elliot, 'so I would ask Old Girls to spare any uniform, especially games wear or red cloaks.' Clothes lists were made as short as possible and one of the items to be dispensed with was the cricket hat which inspired a poem by Margery Pavey-Smith of the Upper Sixth in the *Chronicle*.

O Hat!
Languid and flat.
Who in thy salad days so oft hast sat
Shading with gallant curve the modest brow
Of one who scorns thy erstwhile splendour now.

Ah! now
How sad and how
Battered, debased and bendy-brimmed art thou,
Cast careless in a corner on the floor,
Soiled remnant of the hat thou wast before.

Before!
At tennis or
Casting thy white and shining glory o'er
The cricket-pitch, topping my head with pride,
And falling off if I should bowl a wide.

How wide
Thy brim, to hide
My boiling blushes when I vainly tried
To catch a sitter! In what jocund wise
Playful thou slippest forward o'er my eyes.

Thou flappst my ears no longer as I bat,
Unwept, unhonoured and unremembered hat!

The November Old Girls' Meeting was cancelled because of the danger of travelling to London and at the Summer Meeting many of the Old Girls were in uniform.

Their news included a letter from Betty Rickard (Mrs. Mullan) about her evacuation from Singapore before the Japanese invasion in February 1942. Old Girls' News also gave numbers in the various Services. In 1942 there were 15 in the Women's Royal Naval Service and the following year the number had risen to 33, similarly seven were in the A.T.S. in 1942 and 20 in 1943, 16 in the W.A.A.F. and 31 the following year, and one in the W.A.A.S. in South Africa, V.A.D. three, Naval V.A.D. two, R.O.C two, one in the N.A.A.F.I., M.T.C. two, 12 in various other nursing services and one had joined E.N.S.A.

The first Speech Day for two years was held in 1943 when QAS said good-bye to the staff and pupils of Putney High School who were able to return to London. It was also announced that a small booklet would be produced to mark the 50 years since the school was founded at Caversham, but the important commemoration would be to raise £1,000 for a Jubilee Scholarship Fund.

To the Wednesday afternoon 'War Work' day was added helping at the Babies' Home and Nursery School in Caversham where relays of girls learnt how to change old-style terry nappies without sticking safety pins in their charges, give feeds and take the babies for walks in the large coach-built perambulators. They also dressed and fed the toddlers and older children and played with them. During the term quite a rapport grew up between some girls and 'their' babies. The Juniors also made a Noah's Ark with pairs of animals for the Nursery School.

In summer 1943 QAS pupils joined Kendrick Girls High School for a six-week harvest camp at Harwell, near Didcot. Most stayed a fortnight in relays and helped local farmers harvesting various crops. They went to the Village Technical Institute at Harwell for a canteen and slept in old round army tents in a nearby orchard. These had to be erected by the girls on the sloping ground, who found that the best plan was to sleep with feet towards the central pole but by the end of the night everyone had rolled down the hill and all ended up on the lower side. Girl Guides had put up a row of wash basins on tripods, but these too were on a slope, and as soon as water was poured in the basin tipped and emptied its contents.

There was still keen interest in the Red Cross and 42 pupils passed the Junior First Aid exam Part I with 52 being successful in Part II. For the Junior Home Nursing Exam Part I there were 59 entrants with 45 for Part II and 20 girls completed the Certificate.

School work continued but text books and stationery of all kinds were short. Text books were shared and torn pages carefully stuck together with transparent paper (the forerunner of self-adhesive tapes). All books had to be covered with brown paper to protect the covers.

The quality of ink for the inkwells incorporated in every desk deteriorated so that much work had a grey appearance especially on poor quality paper. Pupils were urged to save and use every scrap of paper, so only small margins were permitted and sometimes extra lines ruled at the top and bottom of the page to squeeze essays into smaller space—thus making the task of staff in marking even more difficult!

Celebrations to mark the Golden Jubilee of Queen Anne's School were muted because of the war. In 1944 the 50th Birthday was marked on Ascension Day by the planting of a tree by the Head Girl, Elizabeth Creswell (Mrs. Bolitho) and a special service in Chapel.

The picnic holiday was not held on the Ascension Day birthday but planned for later. That day in June was remembered by all because of the D-Day landings in France announced on the radio early in the morning. As pupils cycled to the picnic or floated down the river in hired rowing boats, squadrons of planes flew overhead, all going south to Normandy. The celebration ballroom dancing to records in the Hall was curtailed so that everyone could listen to the broadcast of King George VI, the War Report and a service taken by the Archbishop of Canterbury.

The Archbishop, Dr. William Temple, was the guest of honour at the special Speech Day held later in June. In his address he said that the first main object of the Founders of The Grey Coat Foundation had been to provide a training rooted and grounded on Faith. Commenting on the Jubilee booklet written by Miss Elliot, he said that it was 'a cleverly

22.   Tree-planting to commemorate the Jubilee of 1944.

concise history of QAS and the two previous head mistresses). He continued, 'The printed page may show examination successes over the years, but who taught, whose lessons were most vivid, stimulating and enlivened with flashes of humour, which mistresses were loved, and which feared, I cannot find!'

It was also announced that the Jubilee Scholarship Fund has reached its £1,000 target.

Miss Elliot drew her audience's attention to the boards lining the Hall walls and said that of former Head Girls 28 were graduates, two had become headmistresses, two doctors, another was a Vice-Principal of an Oxford college, four were engaged in missionary work, while 27 of the girls had married and produced families—'some of whom qualify by sex for admission to Queen Anne's'. She spoke of the high scholastic standards, the growing music department and other arts such as drama which were becoming more ambitious together with the well deserved reputation for games enjoyed by Queen Anne's especially in lacrosse.

Unfortunately Speech Day was the afternoon after the first rocket bombing attacks on London so news of the progress of the Allies on the Second Front was overlaid by that of deaths and casualties in London and the surrounding area from the new form of aerial bombing.

Speech Day ended with tea in the orchard, which was where the Muriel Hall library now stands, and an entertainment on the Front Lawn. This was *A Midsummer Night's Dream*, with once again a high standard of acting coaxed out of the actresses by Miss Elliot's production. Costumes had to be made from scraps of materials and a great deal of ingenuity was needed to make use of what was available as shortages and clothing coupons meant that nothing new could be used.

Writing in the *Chronicle* Miss Elliot had congratulated the catering staff on the Speech Day tea, especially the delicious cream cakes. The cakes would have been made with dried egg and limited fats. The 'cream' cakes were filled with mock cream. This was made with milk powder, a little sugar and margarine and mixed with tepid water. 'Cream' that could be piped and used as decoration was made with cornflour and milk. These ingredients were boiled and allowed to cool when they were whipped with some sugar and margarine and flavoured with vanilla essence (if available). These 'creams' were so popular that many parents and pupils asked for the recipes!

During the year a permit under War time Building Regulations was granted for the old San in Henley Road to be refurbished as a new biology lab and a large Domestic Science room.

Towards the end of the Autumn Term in 1944 a Christmas sale was held to raise money for the 'Starving Europe' fund. Nearly all the goods for sale were home-made and included toys, dishcloths, brooches, belts, aprons and Christmas cards and calendars. To make sure that these wares could be fairly distributed among the many eager buyers, each

---

A MIDSUMMER NIGHT'S DREAM

PERSONS IN THE PLAY

THESEUS	.. .. ..	..Margaret Wolfit	OBERON	.. .. ..	..Meg Tomkinson
HIPPOLYTA	.. .. ..	.. Pamela Bell	TITANIA	.. .. ..	..Audrey Newman
EGEUS	.. .. ..	.. Mary Bell	PUCK ..	.. .. ..	.. June Preston
HERMIA	.. .. ..	Elizabeth Corner	A FAIRY	.. .. ..	.. Jane Durham
HELENA	.. .. ..	.. Jane Lloyd	PEASE BLOSSOM	.. ..	.. Shirley Fleming
LYSANDER	.. .. ..	Carol Henderson	COBWEB	.. .. ..	.. Diana Turnbull
DEMETRIUS	.. .. ..	.. Margaret Bell	MOTH	.. .. ..	.. Hilary Evans
PHILOSTRATE	.. .. ..	.. Jenifer Lang	MUSTARDSEED ..	.. ..	.. Jean Matheson
ATTENDANTS	.. .. ..	Elizabeth Mackay / Nancy Gore / Susan Pitt-Lewis / Jennifer Kirkbride			
QUINCE	.. .. ..	Valerie Livingstone			June Catnach / Jacqueline Fallows / Elizabeth Giblin
BOTTOM	.. .. ..	Pamela Matheson	OTHER FAIRIES..	.. ..	Gillian Green / Gillian Ord
FLUTE	.. .. ..	.. Diana Bramwell			Judith McGregor / Helen Morfey
SNOUT	.. .. ..	Elizabeth Bowlby			Joan Read
STARVELING	.. .. ..	.. Audrey Overton			
SNUG ..	.. .. ..	Juliet Clutterbuck			

23. The programme for *A Midsummer Night's Dream*.

pupil was given two 'coupons'. At 2.15 p.m. the purchasers were allowed into the sale, but only to inspect the stalls and decide what they were going to try to buy. Then at 2.30 p.m. the sale opened and purchases could only be made by surrendering the two coupons. When everyone had used her coupons, the remaining stock was sold 'off the ration' and nothing was left on the stalls. The afternoon raised over £100 for the Fund.

Even contributions to the *Chronicle* were influenced by the war, with a poem by Margaret Bell about the members of the stirrup pump party and her dream that no one came to help her in the middle of the night, but luckily the 'all-clear' siren sounded before she had to pump the water to put out the flames from an incendiary device. This section also has a photograph of 17 pupils who were daughters of Old Girls.

Two years after the end of the war the Old Girls held a commemorative dinner for 130 at Crosby Hall, Chelsea, and the menu card was illustrated with the many branches of the uniformed Services QAS Old Girls had been in during hostilities.

The following May the long-awaited 'Victory in Europe Day' was celebrated on the evening of Ascension Day when the whole school assembled for a Service of Thanksgiving in the Chapel. The number of pupils had risen with the end of hostilities and the school was now full. The House Michell-Webbe was again divided into two, with a School House and an Out House.

At the 1945 Speech Day Monsieur Varin, Attaché Culturel to the French Embassy, enthralled his audience with an account of his life as a member of the French Resistance Movement. After working for some time he had been caught, imprisoned and condemned to death. He told of his hazardous tasks and how co-operation was an inspiration. After the Prize Giving the seniors gave a display of figure marching and vaulting and juniors performed country dances round a Maypole as well as modern and Greek dancing accompanied by the School Orchestra.

It was also back to the pre-war routine for the second post-war Ascension Day outing, when once again charabancs were hired for the Birthday Picnic at Bisham Abbey. This was followed by a special supper and dancing.

The Old Girls held a Jubilee Thanksgiving Service in the Chapel taken by the Bishop of Gloucester, formerly Canon C. S. Woodward, Chairman of the Foundation until 1933. With the Chapel full, and so many wanting to attend, the Service was relayed by loudspeaker to a large gathering on the lawn.

An entertainment in the Hall was 'The Seven Ages of QAS'. One of the first pupils, Alice Slythe, reminisced about the early days at the newly founded school (see Appendix B). The Head Girl, Marion Glanville (Mrs. Chittleborough) said now the war was over they were allowed to ring both the School bell and the Chapel bell.

In 1944 there were 29 Old Girls who had played in lacrosse internationals and seven were picked for various countries in the United Kingdom as hockey internationals—the winter game re-introduced by the evacuees from Putney High School in which QAS games staff had coached pupils to the same top-class standard as in lacrosse.

As travel restrictions were eased, an Inter Schools Lacrosse tournament was held at Harpenden. The 1st Savs went and competed with 19 other schools. The team scored 42

24. The lacrosse team, 1948/9, included Shirley Crouch, Pat Anderson, Caro Macintosh, June Catnach, Ann Robinson, Jane Ellis, Caroline Robertson, Deborah Brooke, Pat Thain, Rosemary Hatcher and Gillian M. Green.

goals, only conceding one goal, winning the tournament emphatically and starting the many years of success which were to follow.

During 1945 the popularity of hockey was waning especially among the juniors. Only five outside hockey matches were played by the seniors. But both school tennis and cricket teams had successful seasons and a swimming match against the Abbey School, Reading, was won by QAS. At this time the school swimming pool was unheated and the bath was longer and narrower than regulation sized pools. When first filled the water would be clear and icy, but with only basic filtration and cleaning methods, soon became thick and green. The tiny changing cubicles had canvas curtains and each was usually occupied by two or three girls and their clothes and towels.

In 1946 the calendar of events was back to pre-war length with a full programme of lectures during the winter months and games matches with other schools. There was still strict petrol rationing, and those members of staff who had cars had to be careful to hoard their allowance to enable them to give lifts when absolutely necessary.

Two members of staff, Miss Margot Parker and Miss Madge Slaney, played tennis in the Wimbledon competition in the late 1940s. They arranged an Exhibition Match at the school with Davis Cup and Wimbledon players including Dan Maskell and Fred Perry.

Reproduced by kind permission of D. R. Stuart

25.   The tennis team.

The proceeds of another Tennis Exhibition in 1948 paid for the resurfacing of the hard courts. Schoolgirl Pat Thain and her partner won the Girls' Doubles at Wimbledon. She was also in the 1st Crosse team and her Section won the Sergeants' competition. For the first time, as well as set exercises which had been practised for the event, each Sergeant had to teach her Section something during the competition.

At the London Olympics Old Girl, Elspeth Whyte, took part in both throwing the discus and putting the weight—she had broken national records in both these events.

The next year the 1st Crosse won the Inter-Schools Tournament at Merton for the sixth year in succession, beating Queen Margaret's of York 5-1 in the semi-finals (this was the only goal scored against them in the whole tournament) and beating Roedean 4-0 in the final.

More hard tennis courts were laid down in the early 1950s so that the grass courts which were marked out on the Field each summer were no longer needed. The playing surface of these was always bumpy and those lower down the field were on the slope, so that skills of playing up and down hill as well as across the net were gained. There was little boundary netting at the rear so much time was spent collecting tennis balls from the cricket pitches and vice versa. Money for the hard courts was mostly raised at an evening fête, but it poured with rain just as the proceedings opened so sideshows and stalls were hastily moved under cover, with the 80 entrants in the Dog Show parading round the sides of the old 'Swimmer'. The next day, Parents' Day, more money was raised despite the continuing bad weather. The tennis courts were called 'Newbold Courts' in memory of 'Nubby' the former gym and games mistress who came to QAS in 1904, leaving in 1920, but continuing to coach lacrosse and encourage games at School. In 1956 the team from QAS won the prestigious Aberdare Cup for tennis.

The following Spring the 1st Crosse again won at Merton avenging their defeat of the previous year.

In 1957 the long-awaited new swimming pool was opened on a chilly day at the end of May. At the end of the summer term every girl in the School could swim and only three failed 'The deep end' test. Since the new pool was a different length from the old 'swimmer' all School records were set anew.

Clothes rationing continued until 1950 so that it was difficult for full uniform to be maintained, but pupils were given extra coupons by the Government when they first came to school in order to obtain some items. Everyone measured her feet, for once the magic size three had been reached extra coupons were available for shoes.

26. Miss Wheeler, Miss Carter and Miss Reddall.

Food rationing was in some cases more severe than during the war and even bread was rationed. The catering staff, under Miss Carter, had used skill and ingenuity to provide meals over many years. Confectionery rationing continued for some years after the War and the amount allowed per week fluctuated. At one time pupils were allowed to bring sweets from home and these were kept in Matron's Room for School House girls who were permitted to have a few on Sunday after Chapel. Later the School set up a 'shop' so that pupils could buy their own sweets. For School House pupils this was on Saturday mornings after lessons in the sitting room of the Sanatorium. The Houses took it in turn to be allowed into the 'shop' first and buy their permitted four or six ounces (a hundred to a hundred and seventy-five grammes) of confectionery. Stocks were very limited and usually the fourth House members had to make do with a very poor selection, or buy just what remained. When the ration was only four ounces, it was a difficult choice between delicious chocolate that would be gone too quickly, or a less attractive boiled sweet that could be sucked for a long time. For the same reason packets of wine gums or peppermints were popular. The queue of girls would shuffle slowly round the room trying to decide what to buy. For one youngster temptation was too great. She picked up her bar of chocolate near the entrance and by the time she reached the member of staff at the 'till' all she could show for her week's allowance was a crumpled wrapper!

Extracts from letters home by Jennifer Hogarth of Michell show that shortages of basic items and limited choice of food had a big impact on life. This letter was written in 1948. 'For my birthday my best friend gave me—two postcards, an economy label, a piece of tracing paper, a piece of chalk and A SWEET'. The economy label would have been stuck on to an already used envelope so that it could be posted again. With the shortage of any kind of paper, stationery was always useful. Girls who needed new exercise books had to queue up at the Stationery Cupboard where a member of staff inspected the old book and made sure every page had been fully used before issuing a new one.

Another letter home has the plea 'If possible could I have a little margarine for my birthday table?' The weekly butter ration was just two ounces (50 grammes). Each girl's ration in School House would be put into a small screw-top glass jar with her name on top. At the beginning of the week bread, butter and jam could be enjoyed by all, but towards the end those who had been profligate and spread the bread thickly were reduced to begging from others who had shown more restraint. The expression 'buttering up one's friends' took on a very literal meaning. In summer there was a fine art in eating the butter ration more quickly so that it did not turn rancid and inedible in the glass jars which were left in the dining room, while still not being reduced to plain bread by the end of the week. Twice a week a half pound packet of hard margarine would be put on the table, and the House Prefect needed nerves of steel and a steady hand to cut it into 18 exact pieces to enable everyone to have a fair share. That was why it was so important to obtain extra margarine for the bread at a birthday table, so that guests did not have to bring their own butter.

Another letter has a plea for 'apples or something that fills me up'. There were no snacks such as crisps and no canned drinks—but possibly because of this most girls thrived on the spartan diet, obesity was unusual, and, since nearly all were thin and sometimes hungry, anorexia was unheard of!

At the beginning of term Jennifer wrote home, 'I am in trouble because I forgot to ask Mummy for my extra bread coupons to give in to the office'. But she wrote home in triumph later in the term to explain that the English teacher had offered a prize for the best poem. She had won and the prize was a Mars bar—much better than an inedible certificate or cup.

Domestic Science was a popular lesson because the results could usually be consumed at supper and again shared out with others. She writes that she made queen cakes with dried egg and they were not nice. When she made macaroni cheese she put in too much mustard. She was allowed to eat it unheated and solid for supper but comments that it 'was too hot even though it was cold'. One time the lesson was on making apple dumplings with pastry and she and her partner giggled, so the punishment was that their apple dumplings would be served to the staff for supper. But the staff were in for a surprise— under the covering of pastry the cored apple was filled to the brim with cloves and no sugar. However, no further punishment was forthcoming for this revenge.

Another letter contains a request for shampoo. 'It need not be a big bottle that is difficult to post as we are not allowed to wash our own hair and we only get a hair wash four times a term.' This rule was because most children had long hair which was braided into plaits and took some time to dry. In School House a hairdresser came on Wednesday afternoons for 'Wig-Wash Day' to wash the juniors' hair, those with the longest and thickest hair going first. This was so that it would be dry by teatime.

In winter the only method of getting hair dry in School House was for the girls to kneel in front of the gas fire in Matron's (Miss Wheeler's) Room. Somehow no one caught alight, but there was often a nasty smell of singed hair. Also since the hair was brushed forward to dry more quickly many girls left the room with tresses that stuck out in all directions. The school did not appear to own any kind of hand-held or commercial hair dryer. To Miss Wheeler fell the task of trying to keep the girls warm and comfortable during the war, and the period of austerity after it—no mean feat as every day brought new shortages and difficulties; nothing could be replaced and very little repaired.

The organ in the Chapel needed repair and in June 1947 a fête was held to raise the £600 needed for this. The whole organ was overhauled, new pedal boards fitted and an electric blower installed. Luckily the work had not been completed when electricity had to be cut for many hours because of a shortage of fuel in the coldest winter on record. It was decided that the alternative of hand blowing the organ would be maintained for such emergencies.

Generations of pupils had taken their turns in 'blowing', and remembering to get sufficient air in the bellows before the hymn after the sermon was announced. Those learning the organ also had to be prepared to 'blow' for other pupils.

At the Fête a board and ladder were erected outside the office window at the front of the School. A cut-out model of Miss Tyrrell, the organist, was moved up a rung of the ladder every time money was paid into the Organ Fund at the office. By the end of the afternoon she was triumphantly playing the organ at the top of the ladder. That evening Miss Tyrrell gave an organ recital. She was at QAS for 32 years as Senior Music Mistress as well as House Mistress at Wilkins, and House Tutor of Wisdome.

27.   Miss Parkinson and orchestra.

On her leaving A. R. wrote in the *Chronicle*:

> We hymn Miss Tyrrell awefully enthroned
> In lofty splendour, who, with dreadful gaze—
> ('One moment please—my glasses—, now, books up!')
> From raucous throats invokes harmonious lays
> Through many generations. Music's lore
> She taught as well and truly, but in vain
> She strove to teach us who cantoris sang
> And who decani—we forgot again.

Visitors from overseas were now free to travel and teachers came to look round the school from Africa, America, Sweden, India and Denmark, and take back impressions of daily life at QAS. Polish, Rumanian and Chinese tennis players visited to give an exhibition match. German Prisoners of War came to the school to work outside before being repatriated.

In September 1947 the Junior House, Elcot, halfway down Derby Road, was opened for 11 year olds. Two of these first new girls wrote of their impressions in the *Chronicle*. 'The House seemed all passages and stairs and far more than 22 girls. But there were even more girls when we went to the main school the next day for Chapel and Assembly in the Hall and the School too was a maze of corridors'. She wrote how they all felt anxious and frightened as they approached the front door of Elcot and once inside collided with people hurrying about with cases, clothes, books and sheets. Then the girls had their first meeting in the Drawing Room after which they went to their new dorms, each decorated in a different colour, and 'went happily to bed'. A member of Elcot staff recalled that the youngsters automatically joined in all conversations even in those between staff or between staff and visitors at the front door; they showed frank interest in all phone calls! 'However, soon all settled into boarding school life and now look back with amusement on the first few weeks.'

There was an innovation for the Sixth Form, too. Twenty girls were given permission to attend a dance at Pangbourne Naval College. This would be considered normal now but in 1947 it was a rare treat.

Numbers of girls taking and passing the Oxford and Cambridge Higher School Certificate and those taking University Entrance were increasing and more pupils were staying at school in the Sixth form.

1947 also marked the start of the fund in memory of Miss Holmes who had died earlier in the year. The money was to form the nucleus of a Bursary Fund to assist girls in the School.

At Speech Day Miss Elliot spoke of the excellent record of academic and athletic success.

The Speaker, Mr. B. L. Hallward, Headmaster of Clifton and father of four daughters, advocated the return to kindliness and womanly domestic arts while at the same time cultivating a well informed mind. He caused some consternation when he proposed that universities should make their quota for women no higher than 15 per cent.

The Prize Giving was followed by a display of skipping on the Front Lawn. The Purcell opera, *Dido and Aeneas*, was performed in the Hall. The excellent singing and accompaniment of the School Orchestra were noted.

In the Autumn term of 1948, with the newly electric organ playing, the School and Special Choir sang carols and these were recorded by an American company and broadcast over Christmas in Reading, USA.

One task which all School House girls had to undertake was to be on the washing up rota. Jennifer wrote home: 'You think there is a lot of washing up after Sunday lunch but after a hundred plates, a hundred glasses, a hundred side plates as well as pots, pans, dishes and cutlery, then you really know what washing up is!' The washing-up was done in old low lead lined sinks and piled on wooden draining boards with lead flashing. Soda was put in the water to remove grease as washing-up detergent had not been invented!

In fact any kind of hot water was always in short supply—except the kind that naughty children have found themselves in through the years. Baths were rationed to two a week and since there were no showers those whose turn came after Field always had friends who begged for a dip in their water. There was no running water nor basins in any of the dormitories. Every girl had a jug and ewer on the chest by her bed. Each morning as the 'Big Bell' tolled a jug of hot water would be carried through by a maid with a small puddle being doled out into the bottom of each basin. This would be topped up with cold water from the jugs.

After teeth cleaning the dirty water would be carefully lifted off the chest and tipped into a bucket on the floor usually shared between four or five girls. There was a rota to be 'sloppy pail monitress' and empty these buckets. But often the aim between basin and bucket was poor and mopping up was a regular occurrence. On of the popular 'dares' was to swing a half-full pail round and round overhead with such momentum that the water would not spill. That was the theory—some succeeded, others failed—spectacularly!

Most dormitories had curtains to divide the cubicles with their narrow iron railed bedsteads. These were drawn across when dressing or undressing, and many a monitress could creep up and pull the curtains back with a rattle of brass rings to waken any lazy lie-abed or startle a clandestine gathering after 'lights-out'.

In 1948 a party from QAS went to the Commemorative Service for the two hundred and fiftieth anniversary of the Grey Coat Foundation at St Margaret's, Westminster. They had tea at the Grey Coat Hospital, much of which had been destroyed by bombing during the War. Later that year other pupils went to the *Chronicle Play* written, produced and acted by Grey Coat girls in which the foundation of the school by eight Westminster citizens and the granting of the Charter by Queen Anne, and many other events in the Foundation's history, were portrayed.

At this time it was decided to have Speech Day every other year and on alternate years a Parents' Day. In 1949 R. B. writes in the *Chronicle* of this innovation: 'The modern parent is so humble a creature, so browbeaten by his alleged responsibility for all the environmental and hereditary shortcoming of his offspring, so used to being regarded by School authorities as the regrettable but necessary adjunct to his cheque book that he cannot but feel considerable gratitude at the mere recognition involved in an invitation to a Parents' Day'.

Mothers studied iced cakes and well-cut skirts and shorts and fine embroidery while fathers bent over lab benches and relived their early encounters with the internal organs of the dog fish. Displays of schoolwork were on show in form rooms and the lab 'and the charming informality allowed me to spend time with my daughter—a day to win every parent's heart'. There was a short play in French in the Hall, *Half Hour at the Court of Louis XIV* which was 'presented with zest and skill'.

Fathers played cricket and mothers tennis—so perfect was the daughters' hospitality that parents secured well-contested victories. Tea in House gardens or the School orchard was followed by folk dancing—English, Scottish and Portuguese, on the front lawn.

In 1949, 46 girls took School Certificate and ten gained Higher School Certificate, but changes were coming with the introduction of O levels and A levels. The Parents' Day entertainment on the Front Lawn was a mime with six excited dons in academic dress banishing the old examination and heralding the new. Miss Elliot had told parents that this had meant changes in the timetable and syllabus of work and it remained to be seen if the new examination would prove a better instrument than its predecessor which candidates at Queen Anne's had been entering since 1898.

Prefects' Badges could be manufactured again, but they were no longer made of gold. When badges were not available Prefects were presented with 'IOUs' on Speech and Parents' days, and now these could be redeemed and the new brooches of metal gilt in a slightly different design could be claimed.

A German girl, Renate Dramer, came to QAS under a scheme for German children to attend English schools. She wrote of the differences between English and German schooling with its emphasis on high scholastic standards and many examinations. 'I think you have a pleasanter time at school with more leisure than we have. Many of us become nervous as a result of school life'.

Books kept by Heads of Houses through the years are a different type of historical record from the *Chronicle* and official documents in the School archives. The minutiae of exam results, competitions and House triumphs and failures are all recorded through the years. Some contain team and House photos, details of plays performed and their posters and programmes. Others have remarks such as 'behaviour disgraceful—people must realise there is absolute silence before and after Grace'. Manners both at table and towards each other are discussed as well as 'good positions' and those who are a credit to the House and those committing misdemeanours. One thing is consistent whichever House book is read: the uniform type of clear rounded handwriting of early books and the less legible, more individual style of penmanship in later records.

When a General Election was announced, four candidates contested a 'mock election' at QAS and girls showed their political choice with yellow dancing tunics for the Liberals, blue science overalls for the Conservatives and red cloaks for Labour. While the ballot was being held, a party of 'anarchists' staged a mock riot in the Quad. The final figures were Conservatives 190, Liberals 93, Labour 20 and the poor Communist candidate received no votes, not even casting one for herself!

In the autumn term Shakespeare's *The Tempest* was produced by Miss Elliot and a parent writing in the *Chronicle* states, 'it was the only time I ever felt that the shipwreck was a shipwreck and not just a confused noise. The play was beautiful, earnest and real and the production owed a great deal to the vision and imagination of Miss Elliot'.

Whenever Easter was early the Cuddesdon *Passion Play* was performed in the School Chapel under the direction of Miss Elliot and always was a moving and reverent event with excellent music and singing. Throughout her time as headmistress she directed many school plays and there were also lighter moments. When the prefects performed *The Ghost Train* for the staff in the early 1950s no one could place which prefect was the villainous stationmaster until the end of the play when the Headmistress was unmasked! On another occasion she appeared on stage in a sari, took it off, stood unselfconsciously in her petticoat and demonstrated how to put it on. Some of the props, such as the fan, painted in her portrait in the Hall, are from the acting cupboard.

In 1951 instead of an Ascension Day Outing the School visited the Festival of Britain Exhibition on the South Bank in London.

In 1956 a performance of Gilbert and Sullivan's *Princess Ida* was given jointly with Leighton Park School, the boys making the set.

Two teachers took a party of girls to Switzerland as travel restrictions had been lifted. At Berne station they were fascinated by a large chocolate machine requiring no coupons as well as the clock with the bear and delighted in pineapple splits on the way back from the medieval Château de Chillon.

There was a General Inspection in the Spring Term of 1951, the first since 1935. The report commented 'A happy school giving a sound and fruitful education'. Following the constructive criticism of the Inspectors it was decided to turn the ground floor of the San into 'New Library' and the Lower Reference Library (the present Staff Room) into a Reading Room.

The Inspectors also criticised the Sections exercise at Break—'this kind of drill is a little out of date and increasingly unpopular. It has long been discarded by experts and has no particular value'. The Inspectors recommended its cessation after 40 years.

Miss Elliot commented in the *Chronicle*: 'May the future find other ways of enabling QAS girls to learn leadership and acquire poise. 'Lances' (Lance Corporals) have their mettle tested by their Section and many Sergeants have learnt authority and valuable lessons from leading the exercises in the Quad. We will have voluntary country dancing in Break—but what shall we do with the Sergeants Medal?'

At the 1952 Speech Day the girls presented an Elizabethan Pageant in honour of the new Queen Elizabeth. This depicted the visit of Queen Elizabeth I to Reading in 1575, and ended with dancing, including American square dancing. Miss Moore's portrait was presented and hung in the Hall just beyond the platform and she was given a bound and hand written book of the names of all those who had subscribed.

In the autumn of 1952 Miss Elliot took a sabbatical term's leave to go to India, while Miss I. Coleman, Second Mistress, House Tutor and Senior Maths Mistress, who was about to retire, stayed on as acting Headmistress. She had been at QAS for 31 years. Miss Elliot was welcomed back in January 1953 and gave a talk on India. Pupils from the Syrian Christian Girls School at Tiruvella gave six embroidered cushion covers for the Prefects' Room.

Nurse Irvine had also retired at the end of the autumn term 1952 after many years in charge of the San and the School House 'big and little sickers' as well as doling out our pills and potions from her morning Surgery. However, she had to return in the spring term because of a violent 'flu epidemic with over a hundred girls in bed and dormitories taken over as hospital wards. After three weeks Nurse Irvine and 22 members of staff also had the Asian Flu and the School broke up 10 days early.

In 1952 a French Club was started and the main event was a Fancy Dress Ball with costumes from the different regions of France. So many girls wanted to join that the Club had to be restricted to seniors only. At the beginning of the spring term Twelfth Night was celebrated in French style with a 'galette des rois' and the traditional beggar playing the violin and finished with films in French.

The next year the School was closed for five days in June 1953 during the Coronation celebrations. Four flowering trees were planted at School to mark the event and a portrait of the Queen was hung in the dining room above the High Table.

The following year the Governors decided to buy a house on the corner of Derby and Peppard Roads and alter it to house Webbe. Webbe moved in September 1955 and shared kitchens with Maddock. The original Webbe House had been at High View in Derby Road near the top of the field, and plans to build a new house had been mooted since 1939 but permission to build had not been granted.

The Christmas term ended early because a railway strike was threatened and at that time most pupils travelled by train, using the special coaches reserved for QAS between Paddington and Reading at the beginning and end of every term.

In a report of Speech Day 1954 Miss Elliot spoke of high achievements in all fields and said that the new General Certificate of Education brought new problems to a school that aimed at providing a well-balanced curriculum. The former Principal of St Anne's College, Oxford, the Hon. Eleanor Plumer, presented the awards and drew attention to the slow but sure social revolution taking place in Britain and reminded her audience that the Welfare State had its obligations as well as its benefits. Because of rain, tea was held indoors, and many parents were intrigued to watch the Science VIth operating their own distillery.

Mr. Newman who had been Head Porter from 1907 to 1954 retired. He and his wife lived at Newman's Cottage (now the Music Cottage) for 47 years. He would reminisce about the early days when the Quad was barricaded and prison-like with huge gates on either side. The Crafts Room and workshops were shabby farm buildings and gooseberry bushes grew where the Hall was built. The San had been built in an old gravel pit. Before central heating was installed in School House he had to fill 65 buckets with coal every morning and the maids then laid and relit the fires which warmed class rooms, sitting rooms and staff rooms.

By October 1956 the School was raising money for a new outdoor swimming pool and there were plans for new labs, some new classrooms and another library. This year had some notable academic achievements with four of the Sixth Form gaining State Scholarships. The standards in Science were rising every year under the aegis of Miss Lucia, who had struggled for years to teach in the big and little laboratories (the Sykes I.T. centre and room A—now the English book cupboard). Her advice was invaluable in planning the new labs, which were built on the West Wing site where Miss Elliot laid the foundation stone. This was at a time of financial stringency and they form a lasting memorial to Miss Elliot.

In the mid-fifties the School uniform was changed and tweed suits were introduced for Sunday wear.

28.   Mr. and Mrs. Newman.

29.   Miss Elliot laying the foundation stone of Elliot Wing.

Head Girl, Clare Spencer-Bernard (Mrs. Hohler) gave the QAS purse to Princess
Margaret at the Diamond Jubilee celebrations of U.G.S.

Miss Elliot announced at the United Girls' Schools Mission in London that she would
retire at the end of the autumn term 1957. 'It is almost impossible to realise after 19 years
that my time here is coming to an end. The School has for so long been not only my job,
but my home and its members my family. I have such lovely and vivid memories.'
Parents' Day in 1957 was changed to a Speech Day to mark Miss Elliot's retirement and
Mrs. Blair, née Rosemary Allen, chairman of the School Committee, a former Head Girl,
who had had a daughter, Pauline, at QAS, spoke of Miss Elliot's inspiring influence on
the spiritual life of the School.

In April 1958 Miss Elliot went to assist with the Women's Department of the Christian
College in Kottayam, India. She often visited the School and her Old Girls visited her in
her retirement. Miss Elliot died in July 1978. A memorial service was held in October at
Stroud in Gloucestershire where she lived in her retirement. Canon E. H. Tucker, Rural
Dean of Bisley, spoke of her time at Queen Anne's, her love of India working for the
Church Missionary Society and her activities as the Secretary for the Ministry of Women
in the Church.

In the *Chronicle* a tribute read: 'Her interests swept the girls into drama, debates,
discussions on comparative religions, social work outside school and war work'. Another
wrote that Miss Elliot never failed to adhere to high principles and high standards and
sincere Christianity with splendid results for QAS.

Chapter V

The Fourth Headmistress
Miss Challis (1958-1977)

Miss Challis had not even set foot inside Queen Anne's when she accepted the Governors' invitation to be its new Headmistress. As Housemistress of one of the two Sixth form houses at Cheltenham Ladies' College, she did of course know Queen Anne's by reputation and had heard that it was a happy school. Its advertisement for a new Headmistress coincided with a time when her conscience was telling her that, after 12 happy and settled years at Cheltenham, she should be seeking new challenges. At the successful interviews in London, Miss Challis much enjoyed meeting the Governors, and since she did not consider school buildings as such to be important, returned to Cheltenham full of enthusiasm and confidence.

30. Miss Challis with prefects, 1968. Back row, from left to right: Lesley Adams, Anthea Harman, Elisabeth Mardall, Sarah Gibson, Ann Andrews, Juliet Crawley-Boevey, Pauline Jackson, Marion Bellamy, Moira D'Eye, Alison Earley. Front row: Brenda Billington, Celia Spayer, Lesley Oakden, Miss Challis, Ann Mansbridge, Elizabeth Andrews, Anne Stephens.

That summer term Miss Challis went to Caversham to meet the School, her main memory being the presentation of a large bouquet of sweet peas by Goodchild, the Head Gardener. The following autumn term she was invited again by Miss Elliot to stay for two days and learn her way around. Her house at Cheltenham made her promise to do them credit, behave as befitted a future Headmistress, and to wear a hat, so to that end a particularly elegant feathered one was bought and, soon after she arrived, was carried off by Miss Elliot's cat which thought it had captured a very fine bird. Miss Elliot and Miss Faull were simply appalled by this mishap, but the hat's owner was secretly rather relieved that she could revert to a more everyday appearance!

That visit was memorable chiefly for the amount of seemingly indigestible information which Miss Elliot poured out, meetings with the staff and some of the girls, and for the cold. Miss Elliot led a spartan life and there was then not much heating in School. But the warmth and friendliness which met the visitor were unmistakable.

Miss Challis arrived as Headmistress at the beginning of the spring term and made her priority getting to know the girls. By the end of that first term she was able to say goodbye to each one by name. She had discovered several heart-warming factors in her new situation: that the School was the right size, the girls were reasonable and sensible, people spoke the same sort of language, and that, most important of all, the Chapel stood right at the centre and this mattered to the School.

In this spirit, she felt confident to bring in some innovations. At her interviews with the Governors, Miss Challis had expressed her views on freedom: she believed that girls should have as much as they could possibly take, and that it was not fair to release girls into the outside world with no experience of it. They must be allowed contact with the outside world, even if it was only through going on shopping expeditions by bus. And if they could not cope with that, they would lose the privilege until they could. Miss Challis felt there was something a bit old-fashioned about Queen Anne's, that it was rather withdrawn into itself in Caversham, and that there was not enough outside contact. She knew that it was impossible to supervise everyone all the time, but felt she knew the School well enough to know it would not cheat and girls could be trusted to sign books when they were going out, and to be responsible for one another. Against this had to be balanced the views of parents, some of whom did feel their daughters should be closely supervised at all times.

Miss Challis also felt that a Headmistress should be accessible to everyone. Despite a lifelong detestation of the early hours, she made sure that she was in the drawing-room by 7.15 a.m. so that the staff could come in to see her before Chapel if they wanted. Girls came at break, either by 'invitation'—generations of girls will remember that sinking feeling when the Head of School climbed on to a chair in Hall and read out their name, that apprehension being definitely the worst part—or by request at other times. Miss Challis once wondered, on the occasion of a junior bursting in at 6 o'clock one evening to announce that she didn't know the difference between right and wrong, whether this perhaps went beyond the call of duty!

By making a point of teaching all new girls when they came, and others more senior in the School, Miss Challis came to know each one personally. She also met them on social occasions, inviting herself for supper at Houses. It was clear many of the girls were much brighter than they realised, but they were not being stretched. A very high standard of teaching was available to nurture whatever ability there was. She felt supremely confident in her staff. But equally, if girls were not particularly academic, not the sort to pass exams with flying colours, they must be actively encouraged in other areas. The real disaster was dull people leading dull lives. Passionately she believed that people should enjoy their work, or anything else that took their interest. No-one should ever think she was stupid or boring or have no contribution to make. To do this, she turned to her Housemistresses, alternately cajoling and urging them to greater efforts to bring out the potential in every one of their charges.

At her first Speech Day on 28 June, Miss Challis stressed the importance of academic excellence but emphasised good citizenship, and learning to think for oneself. Good citizenship was something to which Queen Anne's has always aspired, and the House reports for each year show how wholeheartedly each one supported charitable causes. When Miss Challis first came, those causes had tended to be the same ones year after year, but she instituted the practice of adopting a particular charity for a year and putting all efforts towards raising a really worthwhile sum of money towards it. In 1960 the School adopted World Refugee Year as their good cause. Some particular favourite causes always received the School's support but generally speaking that support broadened and became more topical as specific needs or disasters claimed its attention. The methods of raising the money, however, remained more or less unchanged throughout Miss Challis' time, with the possible exception of the Sponsored Walk which began in 1969 with the Upper Fifth walking in aid of the Ockenden Venture, raising over £300 in the process. Literally without number were the woollen squares which each House knitted year after year, and which were then sewn into brightly-coloured blankets for refugees. 'But I can't knit!' was considered a challenge in most Houses, and the recalcitrant ones were soon taken in hand and forced to practise until they could.

Then there were House plays, Hallowe'en parties, Christmas parties, fairs and fêtes. These all meant the preparation of refreshments, something which starving schoolgirls were never loath to undertake since toffee saucepans and cake tins always needed to be scraped clean. The results of these labours were sold for touchingly small sums, a penny or so, or perhaps a little more if the entertainment were at the beginning of term and people still had most of their pocket-money.

Societies had always played their part in School life and it was one way in which girls in different Houses, particularly Out Houses, could meet like-minded fellows whom they did not encounter in lessons. When Miss Challis first came, there was a strong Cossacks Society—a cross between a debating and dramatic society—a Scientific Society, whose one annual outing alway seemed to be to Huntley & Palmer's biscuit factory in Reading (very popular since there was lots of tasting to be done) and Le Club Français who wrote precise reports of their ladylike meetings in perfect French: 'Après un excellent goûter dans le jardin nous avons écouté une heure de musique française'. Le Club Français was run by the fascinating Mademoiselle Labbé and Miss Foister who was doubtless the first Queen Anne's mistress to have a Vidal Sassoon haircut, and between them they lived up effortlessly to the girls' idea of cosmopolitan chic. By the end of Miss Challis' time, all these societies had been replaced by many more specialist gatherings which spent much time going on expeditions outside schools, during the course of which they met their contemporaries, both male and female, and had to find their own way there, even if it was only across Reading.

Games were an important part of School life, with lacrosse, played in the autumn and spring terms, perhaps the most serious. Stern were the injunctions in the School *Chronicle*: 'stickwork has been quite good but passing ... has been weak, and needs a lot of practice'; the First XII took 'a long time and several defeats to warm up'; 'play has been rather uneven. There was a tendency to hold on to the ball too long'; junior 'stickwork is not always all it should be', and so on. Nonetheless, the School had a long tradition of winning the South Schools' Tournament at Merton, and it was an unusual year indeed for them not to reach at least the semi-finals. Tennis reached a peak soon after Miss Challis' arrival because of the good luck of having Christine Truman's sister, Nell, in the School. A first-class player herself, she soon collected round her a team which proved to be practically unbeatable and Queen Anne's basked in glory. Under Miss Parker, girls were encouraged to hit balls really hard and put them away! Cricket was played only

31.   Aberdare Cupwinners: P. Rogers, D. Brown, J. Billington, Miss Parker, A. Moeller (Capt.), B. Orchard, L. Parsons.

32.   Sir John Cockroft in the Hall.

until 1961, and few regretted its passing, certainly not the Headmistress. Swimming was definitely for the hearty, since getting into the pool required a determined gritting of teeth, something which improved after 1967 when heating was installed. Swimming colours were introduced in 1961.

In June 1959 The Elliot Wing, comprising a Needlework Room, Physics Laboratory, Chemistry Laboratory, Biology Laboratory, Geography Room, Music Room, Modern Languages Room, Art Room, Library and two classrooms, was ready to be opened officially by Sir John Cockcroft. Miss Elliot herself was unfortunately unable to be present as she was in Kottayam but the School sent her a telegram: ELLIOT WING TRIUMPHANTLY OPENED. The ceremonies started with a short service in Chapel after which speeches were made and an appeal for new books was launched by Miss Challis. This was done in a subtle way: the books in question had already been brought to the new Library and stood there in shining piles. Staff with bookplates, pens (and cash boxes) stood at the ready and so eager were parents to see their generosity instantly recorded that soon a long procession was claiming the privilege of buying a book and presenting it to the new Library. Over £300-worth of books was given to the Library that afternoon alone and still more presented afterwards. Each one was meticulously listed in the *Chronicle*.

Reading and easy access to every kind of book were of the utmost importance to Miss Challis. A well-stocked reference library was indeed essential for all those in the Sixth form, but reading must be encouraged at all levels, for all ages, on as many subjects as possible, including fiction. To that end, she stressed the role of House libraries, and encouraged Housemistresses to persuade their charges to make full use of them. She herself often gave Houses books as presents.

In his speech, Sir John Cockcroft echoed Miss Challis' own views on the remarkable scientific developments which were taking place in the present age. He hoped his audience would not join 'a large majority of our population which looks on science with great fear and disgust as a kind of modern witchcraft'. There should be no divisions between arts and science: as at Queen Anne's 'where science laboratories and library stand side by side, the scientists ... will not neglect the Arts, but will remember that the pleasures of reading are one of the most enduring ... and ... the ability to communicate ... one of the most important accomplishments required for a successful career in life'. He then took a long and enthusiastic tour of the new building, and saw each new room being put to the purpose for which it had been built. In the Chemistry Laboratory, girls were preparing ammonia and chloroform, dissections were taking place in the Biology Department, and somewhere there was a cookery demonstration from which 'fascinated mothers had to be cajoled away'.

Other notable events of the year were the retirement of Miss Watson-Smith, Housemistress of Webbe. One of the 'old school', she not only taught French and German, but took a tremendous interest in each of her girls, getting them reading and undertaking projects. The School chaplain, Canon Mowbray Smith, also retired. He was a weekend chaplain, living in east Anglia during the week from where he brought large quantities of strawberries for summer supper parties to which he invited his favourites. His catchphrase was 'Do have a toffee, they are not fattening', and his flock of schoolgirls always thought of Septuagesima, Sexagesima and Quinquagesima as the traffic lights before Lent! That year a Junior Special Choral had been formed, there had been a virulent influenza epidemic during the Spring Term, so that Maddock became a convalescent home for the duration, and Webbe had given an entertainment during which a conjuror had 'sawn Miss Parker in half and hammered a long nail into Audrey Pretty's head'!

1960 was the year of Prince Andrew's birth which Queen Anne's celebrated with a film and a special supper, '... probably the first time since 1894 that the whole school was treated to chicken!'. It was also the year of Princess Margaret's wedding and Miss Challis hired four enormous television sets which were erected in the Hall so that everyone could see. Father Menin arrived as the new Chaplain and the School quickly took him to their hearts. He had been Vicar of Shiplake, and now moved into the chaplain's cottage in Derby Road so that he was resident throughout the week. This meant he was always available to the girls as someone to approach with problems, and that he was able to introduce a regular mid-week celebration of Holy Communion, which took place on Wednesdays.

The Head Gardener, Mr. H. J. Goodchild, he of the bouquet of sweet peas, retired. Sweet peas were his passion, he showed them professionally, and he loved to discuss them with Miss Challis. Girls, on the other hand, he did not approve of. For one thing, they

33. Mr. Goodchild's retirement presentation. For nearly forty years as Head Gardener he served the school with outstanding skill and devotion, and received the gratitude and best wishes from three headmistresses, Miss Moore, Miss Elliot and Miss Challis, members of their teaching and administrative staff, past and present girls, and his colleagues on the outdoor and domestic staff.

insisted on eating the vegetables he had so skilfully grown. For another, on the rare occasions when they did the weeding, they did it wrongly. He had uncompromising views too on exactly where, exactly what should be planted. 'Not for me to say, miss' or 'it won't do, miss' he would respond tight-lipped to one of Miss Challis' horticultural suggestions and, infuriatingly, he was always right. It was sad that his retirement was so short; he died in August 1961.

That year, the Lower Sixth were taken round the Houses of Parliament by the local Member of Parliament, the First XII lacrosse team reached the finals at Merton but were beaten by St Swithun's, Le Club Français had a stylish Christmas soirée at which 'certaines Upper V mimèrent en ombres chinoises des poèmes de Hérédia et Rostand' and Cossacks held a novel hat-night called 'The Verdict is Yours', in which unsuspecting members of the audience were called upon to defend themselves upon fictitious charges. The jury was the audience and Diana Eade, appropriately as it turned out since she is now a well-known London solicitor, was counsel for the prosecution. Susan Morgan won the Brain of QAS Quiz.

The year had a hilarious end with the staff play, Gilbert and Sullivan's *Trial by Jury* in which Miss Grove played the part of a 'bibulous country yokel', Miss Faull and Miss Thatcher 'somewhat amorous old gentlemen', and Miss Hazel played the piano, with Miss Hatton on the violin, Mrs. Hall-Craggs on the triangle and Miss Challis herself on the drums.

1961 saw the introduction of something different which was to become an annual event in the spring term. Because examinations which had previously taken place at the end of the Christmas term now took place at the beginning of the spring term, there were, as Miss Challis put it, 'some eight days of examinations behind us and eight weeks of work ahead'. This was an exercise in preventing anti-climax. 3 February was declared a special day. In the morning Miss Challis gave a talk on the Greycoat Foundation and the foundation of Queen Anne's. (The School's history was a subject about which Miss Challis had made herself extremely knowledgeable and she had instituted the practice of taking every girl in her Lower Fourth year round Chapel so that she could explain how people were involved, who had given what, and when.) The School then divided into three parts, one third going on a 'musical journey through Europe' with Miss Ascher, one third (juniors) hearing about cookery through the ages and the seniors hearing about church needlework and being shown some beautiful examples. After lunch, people went to Reading's exhibition of local government, heard a talk on religious art, with slides, a recital from Miss Hall-Craggs and Miss Hazel on two pianos, and attended a brains' trust with Miss Challis as the question-master. It was during this event that Father Menin uttered his memorable statement, 'The juvenile delinquent is the greatest discovery of the twentieth century'. The School then sang nursery rhymes in rounds with Miss Leahy and the special day ended with Chapel and prayers for the school. So successful was this special day considered to be that, in subsequent years, the spring term always devoted itself to putting on a fully-fledged Arts Festival which took a slightly different form every year.

This was a year which saw the death of Miss Coleman, known as Jacko, Second Mistress, a mathematician, and Housemistress of Boulte from 1932-52. She came to Queen Anne's in 1921 and was associated with it for over 40 years. She was remembered on Old Girls' Day with a memorial service at which Frances Whidborne (Heaton), Head of Boulte, read the lesson. Frances was later Head of School, another step on the ladder which took her to 'First Lady of the City' as the Press dubbed her: director of Lazard's, director-general of the Panel of Takeovers and Mergers, and first woman non-executive director of the Bank of England.

The Head Porter, Percy Wigmore, died in August. He loved the School and the girls and was one of those people who managed to be everywhere at once, helping heave trunks into cars at the beginning and end of term, always willing.

The School also said goodbye to Miss Faull who was retiring after 40 years' service. She had been Housemistress of Wisdome, then Maddock. She took a great interest in the girls in her House and made them read. She was a good listener, and they could count on her to be strictly fair.

At this time, the juniors lived in Elcot. As Miss Challis felt that the era of great epidemics could safely be declared to have passed, it was decided to convert the old sanatorium, built in the time of Miss Moore, into a new junior House, and to christen it Moore after the School's second Headmistress. Elcot was sold but not before a farewell party to which all ex-Elcots were invited and at which ice-cream was eaten and the current Lower Sixth (Elcot 1955-6) put on a mind-boggling tableau, 'The Israelites building the Pyramids'. A small sanatorium was arranged at Harlech. At the same time, the Old

34.   The staff room.

Swimmer was pulled down and the new Arts and Crafts block erected in its place. The Craft Room contained potters' wheels and a kiln and suddenly making pottery became all the rage. It also contained a medical room (scene of the dreaded 'flu jab' queue—rumour had it that one girl had not moved on smartly enough and received two jabs in the arm) and the Bursar's office. Generations of girls had practised banging tennis balls on the wall of the Old Swimmer, so a new banging wall was built at the back of Moore.

High points of the year were the school play, Sheridan's *School for Scandal* produced by Miss Cooper for Parents' Day in June, the adoption by Boulte juniors of a young blackbird, Sydney, which took up permanent residence inside the House, the Nativity Play written by Christine Eade for Cossacks entitled *Christ Our Saviour is Born*, the formation of an Art Society which went to the Tate to see an exhibition of Toulouse-Lautrec, and a special trip to London to present to the captain and crew of the merchant navy vessel, the *M. S. Goulistan*, a library of books for which the School had raised the money in

35.   Miss Moore with the first Moore House, Miss Thatcher and the last girls in Elcot.

Chapel collections. Miss Tucker took four of the Lower Sixth to present the books in person and they had a wonderful afternoon being shown around the vessel, given tea, and lastly travelling through Chinatown, 'a part of London hitherto unknown to us'!

1962 was marked by a fire in the Elliot Wing, fortunately short-lived with negligible damage. Unfortunately, it happened just as the Lower Fifths were decorating the Hall for the Bust-up and the school was deprived of light and heat for over two hours. Electricians managed to install a temporary transformer and the party went ahead as planned. Moore was now properly settled into the new House and received a visit from the bearer of its name who told them about Queen Anne's in her time as Headmistress. She presented them with a book for their library.

Miss Slaney, Head of History, inspiration of Sixth form historians, excellent golf player and keen gardener, retired. The School lost two more stalwarts: Harry Grantham, the school carpenter, always helpful, always jolly, origin of many a good story, and Nurse Duffus, who had come to help with a measles epidemic and stayed 11 years, both died and were remembered in prayers. The Bishop of Reading introduced the School to the

Twentieth Century Folk Mass written by the Rev. Geoffrey Beaumont and, although resistant at first, soon '... strains of the Beaumont Folk Mass could be heard issuing from the bathrooms all over Queen Anne's'. In June, the Special Choral took part in what was to become an annual event, the School Choirs' Festival at Winchester Cathedral. Miss Cooper had another success with *The Lady's Not for Burning* by Christopher Fry in which leading parts were played by Charlotte Crichton, Ann Wilson and Caroline Albery (Johnson).

Much of that year's fund-raising was devoted to the Tennis Court Fund which needed £1,055 and by the end of the summer term the School had raised £835. Webbe held a dance in the Olympia Ballroom in Reading, and Wisdome held a fair in the Hall. The Staff always joined wholeheartedly in fund-raising projects and produced a home-made panto-mime for the Tennis Court Fund. Later, when the swimming pool needed to be deepened, they put on an entertainment during which—for probably the first and only time—a Queen Anne's Headmistress appeared on stage in a grass skirt!

Societies were busy with various activities. Posy Simmonds began a new one called Appreciation of the Visual Arts Society, which was broadly based and showed films and gave lectures to all aspiring art enthusiasts, but whose most popular meeting was a Painting to Jazz session, at which 'A great deal of paper, a great deal of paint and a great deal of splosh absorbed everyone's energy, as they translated Bilk, Barber and Bechet into pictorial form'. This was perhaps one of the first public manifestations of Posy's great initiative and originality which has led to her great success as a cartoonist. The Scientific Society had a more exciting year than usual, making a model of the human eye out of a goldfish bowl, and watching Miss Lucia making a miniature rocket in the Physics Laboratory. The Dramatic Society held a poetry reading at which Webbe 'disguised very convincingly as tombstones' read a collection of poems of death 'most of which were very funny'!

The following year (1962-3) was summed up as one of skating triumphs and boiler failures. It was the winter of the Big Freeze and most of the School spent most afternoons up at Caversham Park skating on the big lake. The grand new heating system proved very uncertain, even when the porters understood that when the controls said 'Off', they meant 'On', and vice versa. It was also a year when government inspectors came to look at the School; they were very friendly, however, and took their meals in the dining-room and chatted to the girls about anything from politics to beetles so that everyone rather enjoyed their visit. They watched the First XII in action on the field and thought they were easily as spectacular as Tottenham Hotspur at White Hart Lane.

Miss Stert retired after a lifetime devoted to Queen Anne's. Meticulous in her approach to everything she undertook, whether it was teaching French, gardening or letter-writing, she was much appreciated by her House, Ffyler, who were very sad to lose her, as were all her friends in the Staff Room.

That year the chosen charity was Freedom from Hunger Campaign, for which the School raised £300. The autumn term was enlivened by a week's visit from Father Denis of the Order of St Francis. He spent one day in each House and took Divinity lessons. The School held a Music Competition in the spring term. Because of the weather, there was no lacrosse for six weeks, but the First XII still managed to reach the semi-finals at Merton, but were beaten by Benenden. The tennis First VI won the coveted Aberdare Cup which was awarded to the best team from all English girls' schools, maintained and independent. Societies were busy, with the Art Society holding a Ban-the-Bomb painting evening, the scientists staining dogfish muscle which 'was more difficult than it looked', and the formation of a new Bridge Club.

The following year (1964-5), Miss Moore's 90th birthday was celebrated. Miss Challis took the Head of School, Alison Moffett and the Head of Moore, Margaret Harvey, in one car and Miss Leahy (who had been at Queen Anne's in Miss Moore's time) and Miss Grove went in another. They took Miss Moore out to lunch in Oxford and presented her with carefully considered tributes which included cards, flowers and fruit grown in School, a cake decorated with the school crest on top and red-cloaked figures round the side, essays written by girls in Moore, a calendar with photographs of Moore, an item of pottery made in the Craft Room, and a photograph album. The Old Girls contributed a bottle of champagne.

Camden, formerly a staff house, was converted into a senior house for eight girls. They enjoyed such luxuries as spring mattresses and reading lamps. This was a pilot scheme in Miss Challis' grand plan of starting a Sixth Form House where girls in the Upper Sixth would live in more relaxed and less supervised surroundings, where they could be encouraged to organise their own working patterns, and to be more independent, away from a highly structured routine. By starting in a small way with Camden, Miss Challis hoped to show her Housemistresses that such a scheme could work. The lucky first eight girls were chosen by reference to those Housemistresses who suggested people who would most benefit, probably girls who were going to university, and to whom this would be a foretaste of their new life. It turned out to be a great success, even those members of staff who questioned the 'luxuries' agreeing that it had not permanently spoilt anyone's character.

That year's charity was Save the Children Fund and the Houses were as busy as usual with their fund-raising activities. Wilkins and Ffyler combined to raise £70 for the victims of Skopje and many more squares were knitted for refugee blankets. In Chapel, some experiments with new forms of worship were taking place and some hymns had new settings. The Carol Service had a 'less sentimental approach' with the lights remaining on throughout. Lacrosse and tennis had successful seasons and societies continued to flourish. A new one, the Fashion and Beauty Society, was much concerned with its members' figures. Miss Parker conducted some keep-fit classes and they were given a lecture from which they were doubtless relieved to hear that 'our Sunday lunch contained the right amount of calories'. Since in Ffyler at least, Sunday pudding consisted of a pink fluff appropriately called Vacancy, this was probably correct! The Photographic Society under the aegis of Miss Ponting had an exciting time 'shutting one another up in a cupboard under the stairs' in an attempt to learn developing, and those who belonged to the C.E.W.C. heard lectures on Indonesia, unilateral disarmament, the need for British leadership in world affairs, and the aims of the United Nations. Their social work projects involved decorating old people's homes. Le Club Français held an evening of charades 'qui a couté beaucoup d'effort mental'.

In her report in the *Chronicle* for the next year, Miss Challis was at last able to describe the progress of her new Senior House, 'taking shape in a sea of mud'. It was a project in which she herself was very closely involved. There was more change in the running of the School by the formation of a School Council. This was a democratically elected body of representatives from each year except the Upper Sixth who were left free to work for A levels. At the first meeting, the topics under discussion were School charities, Chapel services, societies and leisure activities, and arrangements for the School party and Ascension Day. Members were certainly enthusiastic and full of ideas, but some felt there was a lack of response from the School, particularly when it came to making constructive suggestions for improvements. There was also a Chapel Committee which had a representative from each House and met Miss Challis twice a term with suggestions from their respective Houses. Another of Miss Challis' wishes was being realised: less isolation from the community of Caversham. Links with St Peter's were established, with the whole School atttending an Advent Carol service and a family communion service on Whit-Sunday. The school had also become involved in the Caversham Youth Stewardship Campaign, and visited old people and baby-sat.

Discussions about the School party led to the institution of a Christmas weekend. Queen Anne's had always had a party, the Bust-up, on the last Saturday night of the Christmas term, followed by a Carol Service on the Sunday, but now these two main events were enveloped in a proper Christmas weekend in which everyone participated, and which meant a great deal to many girls. On the Saturday, the School was decorated and Christmas cards were delivered. In the evening, the Bust-up, which had originally been a dance (at which girls danced with each other and with the Staff: heads of form could be seen rushing about, their form mistresses' dance cards in hand and a desperate expression on their faces for days beforehand, 'Come on, someone's got to dance with Thatch!') became a more general entertainment with each House doing a turn. On the Sunday there was corporate Holy Communion, followed by the Lower Sixth nativity play. The School then indulged in a large Christmas dinner and the weekend reached its climax with the Carol Service during which a special collection was made as the School's Christmas present for some special cause or someone in particular need. Then, after a light supper, Miss Challis read poems and prose extracts on a Christmas theme to senior girls.

That year, a Library Survey conducted by the Lower Sixth discovered that 16 per cent of girls turned down the corners of pages as book marks and that most of the School were in favour of inter-House library lending. Ffyler was only prepared to agree if a system of fines could be imposed for miscreants! In the spring term, there was an inter-House Music Competition, won by Boulte and Maddock, and another competition called Projects in which everyone, either individually or in small groups, had to make something original, using as much ingenuity as possible. The results ranged from an exact model of Chapel, including 'Twink', all the pictures, and stained glass, to a chess set carved from salt, and a map of the world showing where each girl in the school lived. The first lacrosse and tennis teams had a brilliant year, winning Merton and the Aberdare Cup, though House matches in swimming had to be abandoned because of the poor weather. The Art Society were pleased to be asked to make pottery figures for the new nativity crib at St Peter's, the Fashion and Beauty Society continued to worry about its waistline, and the Music Society sang *Noye's Fludde* by Benjamin Britten.

36.   Michell, Miss Ponting and Mrs. Bidder.

Autumn 1966: at last the new Senior House was 'triumphantly in occupation', although the official opening did not take place till the Summer Term when it was performed by one of the School's most distinguished Old Girls, Lady Brooke of Ystradfellte. Miss Challis had consulted with senior girls about the sort of accommodation they wanted, and they had said they would like a mixture of single and double rooms, and these had been provided. Every bedroom had a desk and each room was individually furnished. Down-stairs, there were two sitting-rooms, a kitchen and a small library, all reasonably spacious.

Looking back, Miss Challis attributed the enormous success of the Senior House to its three excellent Housemistresses, Miss Ponting, Miss Wheeler and Mrs. Bidder, all of whom understood the desirability of letting people grow up and, within bounds, 'do their own thing', to use the current idiom. Girls were individuals and each one wanted something slightly different. They had to learn to live together, work together, cook together and even entertain together. For that was one completely new element of freedom, being able to go out with their friends, and invite them back, unsupervised—as long as they were friends of whom their parents knew and approved.

With the Upper Sixth now completely out of the main school buildings, Miss Challis turned her attention to reorganising School House into just two houses, Boulte and Wisdome. Holmes had moved to Camden and Michell was the name of the Senior House. Before this, all four Houses had been mixed up together, mixed in their dormitories and sitting-rooms and, to girls in Out Houses, seemed not like individual Houses at all. Now they each had a separate identity, and their own Housemistress on a par with Out House Housemistresses. Miss Challis had always disapproved of the practice of School House Housemistresses being somehow lesser beings 'promoted' to Out House Housemistresses.

Wisdome now had the west side of School House and Boulte the east. Each had a quiet room, a large main sitting-room and another senior sitting-room. In the dining-room, smaller tables were arranged so that civilised conversation was possible. Outhouse people had always said good-night to their Housemistresses and this became the practice in Wisdome and Boulte. 'As a result of all these changes', recorded the *Chronicle*, 'everyone has found that there is far more of a family atmosphere and everyone feels part of a House much more than previously'.

With Holmes now in Camden (renamed Holmes) housing some senior girls, with the rest in the new senior House, Michell, the names of the eight Founders were still in place, attached to separate Houses.

The move to Michell was the appropriate moment for Miss Grove ('Air G'), Housemistress of the old Michell, to retire. She had been at Queen Anne's for 33 years, and her association with it was to continue until her death in 1991. Generations of girls had learnt geography and mathematics with her and her catchphrases were legion: the most famous being, 'Watch the board while I go through it'! Father Menin also retired, to the sadness of the School.

This was the first year of the fully-fledged Spring Term Arts Festival. Juniors in each House produced part of a play, without help from their seniors, and each House also presented a short, well-known piece of music treated in an original way. There was also a prize for an individual entry: a drawing, painting, flower-arrangement, piece of original prose, verse or music composition.

It was also the first year of a whole series of new activities, some of which were classed as games and took place in the afternoon, and others which were more like the old societies, which took place in the evenings. In the former category were Athletics, Judo, Fencing and Modern Ballet and in the latter, Bell Ringing, a Handyman Course run by Major Fife who was reputed to have had seven cars and five wives. After theoretical instruction, the class began to dismantle an Austin Seven. The old societies continued in

37.   Miss Grove—'Watch the board while I run through it'.

much the same form, the Photography Society members still perched on fire buckets in the cleaning cupboard in pitch darkness trying to develop their films. There was a new Current Affairs Society which met weekly and discussed the topic of the moment. News items and articles were then pinned on to the board for the benefit of the whole School. Unfortunately this public service lapsed after a couple of terms as no-one had time to do it properly.

In the spirit of change which was sweeping through Queen Anne's at the end of the decade, the 1967-8 *Chronicle* was edited by a member of the Sixth Form, Lesley Oakden, assisted by a group of senior girls and advised by a member of staff. Not surprisingly, it had a younger slant and there were many original contributions from the School, as well as more photographs and line drawings. Perhaps Lesley found this and her time as Head of School a useful preparation for her present work as a television producer.

There was a tribute to Miss Chesterman who had retired, but it did not mention the inspiring but somewhat idiosyncratic way in which she taught Shakespeare, which she read out loud to her class. When she encountered parts which she regarded as in any way improper, she simply omitted them altogether. Consequently, the class was often several lines behind her, pondering deeply about what exactly was so unsuitable for young minds. She had been at Queen Anne's for 21 years and both her Houses, Boulte and Wilkins, were devoted to her. Miss Parker, who had presided over so many famous victories, also left. Her great strengths were lacrosse and tennis for both of which she was an unequalled coach.

The School Council had decided on a new policy for charities: that a special charity should be chosen each term as a focus for the School's efforts, but that regular help to their favourite old-established causes would continue. These were an eclectic lot: the Save the Children Fund, the Merchant ship *M.S. Goulistan*, Christian Aid, Help the Aged, Oxfam, Guide Dogs for the Blind and the Shaftesbury Society. The School managed to raise an amazing amount of money in their time-honoured ways (penny fairs, films, volunteer gardening, sweet-making, sports and competitions): £111 for the European Campaign for World Refugees in the Christmas term, over £250 during the spring term. It was surprising they had time left for anything else at all.

But this year, like all the others, was crammed with activity. The School put on an opera, *The Happy Prince*, by Malcolm Williamson. There was a Lower Sixth dance with Wellington, Bradfield, Reading School and Pangbourne. There was a Poetry Reading with real live poets in the spring term. The First XII won at Merton, lots of girls took bronze and silver examinations in judo, volley-ball was taken up, as was golf at the Emmer Green course which lent witness to the fact by several embarrassing slashes on the turf, and squash began for the Upper Sixth.

Miss Challis had been busy as a committee member on the Boarding Schools' Commission which was asking two main questions: should we have boarding schools and should girls go to boys' schools? She was also an executive committee member of the Association of Headmistresses, one of only two from independent schools. They were concerned with what was to happen to public examinations, particularly A levels. The result of all this consultation was to make everyone far more self-conscious, more aware of advantages as well as disadvantages. One of the apparent advantages of Queen Anne's was how close-knit the School community was, one example being the return of Miss Stert and Miss Grove to help out on a temporary basis in the absence of full-time members of staff.

Another advantage of independence was that the governors gave the Headmistress a free hand so that in those pre-National Curriculum days, she could vary what was undertaken and the amount of time spent on various subjects. The value of academic work could never be over-emphasised but there was more to life than examinations. The Spring Term Arts Festival was one manifestation of this belief and it went from strength to strength, with everyone in agreement that she had broadened her outlook. That spring, the Festival included an inter-House drama competition by the Lower Fifths downwards, an inter-House music competition by one of their number and a public-speaking competition. There were also opportunities for girls to submit art and craft entries, all of which were later sent to the Save the Children Fund.

New building at Queen Anne's never stopped. This year's cause was to deepen the swimming pool. The previous summer all competitive diving had had to stop because the pool was officially declared too shallow. Expert advice was taken. A concerted effort by the whole School was so successful that it raised enough money for the newly-deepened pool to be opened officially the following Parents' Day with a short swimming and diving display.

Witness to Miss Challis' aim to give increased opportunities for senior girls to acquire independence and think for themselves was the number of expeditions they had started to undertake, mainly connected with their own subjects, but also social engagements and singing and drama engagements with other schools in the area. Girls went to the Ideal Home Exhibition at Olympia, *King Lear* at Cheltenham, the Allegri Quartet at Reading Town Hall, *The Merchant of Venice* at Bradfield, *The Taming of the Shrew* at Stratford, and Euripides' *Hippolytus* at the Cambridge Arts Theatre. Those taking A level Economics went to Pressed Steel Fisher at Cowley and Sixth Form scientists to the Science Museum and Faraday Lecture. The Senior Singing Group and the Special Choral participated in a concert of sacred music at Wellington College. Earlier that year they had taken the female parts in the College's production of *Post Horn Gallop*. One girl recorded, 'Occasionally we felt that the half-mile walk to Reading station and the nerve-racking ordeal of trooping up Wellington drive were just not worth it!'

Miss Moore died on 29 April 1969 at 94 years of age. The School held a Memorial Service for her on Old Girls' Day, 28 June. The Special Choral sang 'How Lovely are Thy Dwellings Fair' by Brahms and Mrs. Blair, Chairman of the QAS Committee, gave the address. In more permanent memory, the School decided to build a recreation room on to Moore. This was officially opened on Speech Day 1970. A fine pair of Memorial Doors into the Chapel was also erected in her memory.

Had she lived to see it, Miss Moore would have been one of the most enthusiastic guests at a special celebration, called Queen Anne's 1894-1969, held on the last night of the summer term to celebrate the School's 75 years in Caversham. Each House produced a musical item, for example Maddock sang of the School's motto, and Boulte about the Foundation's history in a calypso. Then the two senior Houses recalled high spots from the history of the School, such as the celebration of the relief of Pretoria when staff and girls, wearing patriotic cockades in their hats, marched round the field singing, 'Rule, Britannia'. A 75th Anniversary Art exhibition was held in the Studio and that year's celebration of the School's birthday on Ascension Day had included a visit from girls from Grey Coat Hospital who were shown round the School and stayed for the evening party when a 75th birthday cake was cut.

Miss Thatcher retired at the end of term. To each and every new girl in Moore, she had been the comforting figure half way between home and school. She had a knack with them, knowing how to keep them on an even keel and getting them settled in. She was kind and completely fair, and always prepared to listen to them. She was deeply religious; she belonged to the Third Order of St Francis, though the School was unaware of this.

Changes were taking place in Chapel—different years were taking turns to arrange special Sunday evening services and the Houses arranged morning chapel on Fridays, though optional evening Chapel with a quiet service of reading, prayer and meditation continued. Girls were giving more help to the old and handicapped in Caversham. They helped at a club for the elderly, making tea, talking, singing to guitars. They also made home visits where they made themselves useful by polishing floors, cleaning brass and hoovering carpets. Sixth Form volunteers also went to Battle Hospital to help in geriatric wards, physiotherapy departments and the cerebral palsy clinic.

Inside Queen Anne's, the Spring Term Arts Festival included a Choral Speaking contest, and folk songs. There was a Sixth Form Conference on human rights in Africa, attended by nine other schools. Expeditions included a sponsored walk in aid of Oxfam, abandoned at lunchtime because it was so boiling hot, a visit to the House of Commons by the Lower Sixth economics and public affairs group and a two-day visit to Leeds University to discover what was available from a 'provincial' university.

There seemed to be no end to it: a conference at Reading School on Religion: Invention or Discovery?, a folk happening at St Luke's Church, Reading, 32 of the Sixth Form attending a World Health Conference and discussing food shortages in developing countries, a Sign-in on World Poverty, a Feed-in folk evening, singing the Verdi *Requiem* at Bracknell Sports Stadium with Wellington. Even Moore was taken to the Planetarium and Madame Tussaud's (where they were impressed with a waxwork of Prince Charles, but less so by the wives of Henry VIII, 'very ugly with rich heavy clothes on'). Even to those who had been at Queen Anne's less than 10 years earlier, it seemed amazing that so much independence and freedom had been achieved in so short a time, and with such encouraging results. They were not frivolous expeditions, but neither were they all deadly, a fine mixture of the topical, subject-related, religious, charitable and social.

The 1971 Spring Term Festival had three sections: Music and Drama, Art and Reading, and Practical—each House had to produce a doll dressed with several garments. The first section was won by Boulte with an extract from *The Jungle Book*, particularly impressive since only school uniforms could be used as costumes. There were several other dramatic productions that year: the Junior Dramatic Society put on *Toad of Toad Hall*, produced by Miss Challis, Webbe put on *Quality Street*, Moore *Flax into Gold*, Wisdome *The Housemaster*, Ffyler Arthur Miller's *The Crucible* and, at the end of the summer term, the Upper Sixth did *Pride and Prejudice*. The character of Mr. Collins aroused strong feelings in the audience!

Miss Challis had always been keen to promote Careers and in her time a Careers Room was opened, plentifully supplied with leaflets and books about what was available, where to do it, what qualifications were needed to do it, how to go about finding out about it and so on. There were also staff about to consult. This year started a regular practice of Old Girls coming back to School to talk about their own careers. Hilary Forrester-Paton talked about occupation therapy, Ashley Moffett about medicine and Inneen Young about being a solicitors' articled clerk.

It was with great sadness that the School said farewell to Mrs. Blair, Chairman of the Governors since 1963, who retired at the end of the summer term. She marked her retirement with a farewell visit to the School and the School responded by entertaining her for practically every minute of her waking day. And when the girls gave up, the staff took over. The formal part of her visit was the unveiling of a commemorative plaque at the foot of a new flagstaff. The School sang a specially worded song. She was invited to meals at every House, and each form then entertained her: the Lower Fourth with spirited extracts from *A Midsummer Night's Dream*, the Lower Sixth with Gilbert & Sullivan's *Trial by Jury*. Among her presents, she was given a special Queen Anne's doll complete with the entire School uniform prescribed by the Clothes List. The last evening, the whole

School and 400 parents gathered in the Hall to hear Miss Challis speak of her good sense, her determination that the best of Queen Anne's tradition should be upheld, and that new achievements should constantly be attempted. She spoke of Mrs. Blair's refusal to give in to prospects of financial gloom, her unstinting gift of time and interest in the School's service. Miss Challis herself owed her a personal debt of gratitude for her unfailing support, especially in reforms to the School, and in educational theories and practice. It was with an appalling sense of loss that she faced Mrs. Blair's retirement.

In her reply, Mrs. Blair made it clear how much the School owed to its Headmistress. They had had no doubt they were following the best course in leaving her a free hand and in seeing their role as a background one. Certainly in her time as Chairman, Queen Anne's had undergone huge changes: in the buildings themselves and in the way in which the School was run. They had achieved this happy state of affairs very much as a team, seeing eye-to-eye on all the main issues.

It had been a packed year, as usual. Chapel had been redecorated with red and white walls, and, with the Moore Memorial Doors now matched with a Frontal Cupboard in memory of Father Menin, and flower stands in memory of Miss Eyles, Matron of Ffyler (1958-66 and of Wisdome 1966-70), looked quite different. There had been an experiment to end the compulsory full School service on Sundays (though each girl had to attend one service on a Sunday) but this had been thought to be a mistake as the School missed worshipping as a community. Anyone who could sing or play had had a full year, with the Special Choral singing at Dorchester Abbey, and the Senior Choir at Bracknell with Wellington. The Arts Festival in the spring term had demanded a musical ballet with live music from each House.

No musical event at Queen Anne's, particularly associated with Chapel, could possibly have occurred without Miss Leahy. An Old Girl and a contemporary of Miss Challis at Cambridge, she was a person of infectious enthusiasm. Who could forget her standing on the Chancel steps during Choirs on Saturday morning, expressive hands darting up and down with the music, her head thrown back in concentration, spectacles twinkling? That weekly practice ingrained hymn tunes and anthems for life. And at the Carol Service every year she created a unique blend of the traditional and truly original.

There had been more investigation into careers: the Lower Sixth had attended a series of lectures at Reading University, on computing, medical research, the civil service, and personnel. There were lectures on career possibilities for linguists, scientists, and banking, in the unexpected form of the young and athletic Mr. Pitcher, the assistant manager of Barclays Bank, Caversham who bounded on to the platform and apparently kept his audience spellbound. Two Old Girls, Catherine Venning and Frances Lowe, returned to talk about teacher training at Homerton and engineering respectively. Frances had actually worked on Concorde.

This was the year of the three-day week, so it was by candlelight that Boulte prepared for the Radley school dance. In the spring term, the postmen went on strike, practically provoking a retaliatory one at Queen Anne's in protest. Life at boarding school is hard indeed without letters. Everyone was busy raising money—this time for new squash courts. Boulte put on *Peter Pan*, and undertook weeding campaigns. Ffyler went one better and persuaded the Bursar that he must pay them Juvenile Agricultural Rates for their gardening efforts! Wisdome held a bridge and whist evening and a swimming gala, at which Miss Challis drew the raffle tickets. She managed to win for herself a 2lb box of strawberries, but her offer to re-draw the winning ticket was refused by the whole School. Webbe held a dog show to which parents and friends brought all shapes and sizes of dogs, who mainly disobeyed all commands given them by the judge, and Maddock held a barbecue with guitar music and gypsy fortunes.

The field had always been a focus for School activities so it was with some sadness that the Headmistress and Governors saw the inevitable widening of the Henley Road. The scheme involved the felling of several much-loved trees on the boundary, and for a time the School felt very exposed before the new fence was erected and a hedge and several new trees planted. It also meant the loss of some of the field itself, for which the School was compensated. It used the money to build a new Cookery Room. Miss Challis was determined to keep the old market garden on the other side of the road, though it was some time since the School had grown its own vegetables. Reading Council was very keen to buy the land and develop it but Miss Challis wisely ensured that it was retained by the School. They built some more tennis courts on it, as well as a little house for one of the gardeners, that way retaining planning permission should need arise in the future for further building. The land is also used for additional car parking when required.

The following year two 'giants of the past' died, Miss Faull and Miss Thatcher. Miss Faull was remembered in Chapel on Old Girls' Day. She had come to Queen Anne's in 1921 and had been Housemistress of both Wisdome and Maddock. In her will, she left Queen Anne's the money for a new Junior Reference Library, which bears her name. The School remembered her with a rose-bed and inscribed bird bath. The School also had to contend with the retirements of two further giants, Miss Ponting and Miss Ascher. 'Pont' was renowned for her ability to throw a piece of chalk backwards over her shoulder at any girl suspected of day-dreaming, the trick being that she could see the dreamer's reflection quite clearly in her spectacles, and also for the poetic descriptions she brought into her subject, biology. She had been a much-respected senior Housemistress. As for Miss Ascher, hers was a character of infectious enthusiasm, of undertaking all enterprises with zest. Whether she was playing at the Wigmore Hall or to one or two in her own home, she put everything she had into it.

The School had lost its chaplain, Mr. Stacy Waddy and for the autumn term was without one. Clergy from neighbouring parishes had been very kind, but it was not quite the same thing, so they were relieved when the Rev. Neville Smith (inevitably known as Rev. Nev.) joined them in the spring term, and was inaugurated by the Bishop of Oxford.

The Arts Festival had an historical bias with the result that everyone felt she had learnt something about different periods of history, and the School's charity was Cancer Research. There was much voluntary service in and around Reading: Sixth formers went to Battle Hospital on Wednesday afternoons and with Leighton Park produced a Christmas party for old people. Girls also went to Borocourt Hospital. There was a Starvation Lunch to raise money. In May some of the school attended a speed reading course and found that, though normal reading speed was only 300 words-a-minute, after two hours, some had reached 800 words-a-minute!

Miss Challis gave a lecture with slides on early civilisations in Crete, Lesley Oakden returned to talk about stage-management as a career, but the most memorable event of the year was doubtless Miss Challis' production of Dorothy Sayers' *The Zeal of Thy House* in which a starring role was taken by Jenny Seagrove as the Archangel Michael, an early success for a well-known actress today.

The year 1973-4 saw experiments in Chapel with the Series 3 form of communion (but the School decided it preferred Series 2). There was a memorial service for Miss Thatcher, with readings and prayers associated with St Francis. The Arts Festival had a literary bias. The chosen charity was Spastics and the School entered the Spastics' National Schools Competition which they then proceeded to win, having raised £2,361, over £7 per head. The prize was a colour television which they decided to give away, to the Bonhomie Old People's Home at Hurst, near Twyford. This was a new establishment which the School had 'adopted', and it had no television set. As a reward for their hard work fund-raising, Miss Challis gave the School a half day's holiday, which was tacked on to the following autumn half-term.

The generosity of the girls with the support of their parents was even more admirable when taken in the context of the unprecedented rise in fees. Queen Anne's had never been intended by its Founders to be a School for the very rich, and the Governors and Miss Challis were absolutely determined to do everything in their power to ensure that the School continued within the reach of parents of moderate means. If economies were made, it was not apparent from the record: in the 1974-5 year nearly 500 new books were added to the three School libraries, and Queen Anne's acted as hostess in a number of local events, including debates with other schools, the Christian Forum, and entertaining old people from the Bonhomie Home to tea. They also continued to make exciting excursions: some even heard Jeremy Thorpe in a 'bright orange luminous coat' speaking 'tremendously well' at a Liberal meeting and in the Easter holidays some of the Sixth form went to a conference at St Catherine's College to discuss world population growth, communes in China, and the world oil supply and Arab politics, before dashing out into the Oxford dusk to explore.

That summer term the School put on a performance of the Wakefield Cycle of Mystery Plays on Parents' Day. Since this took place on the Front Lawn, and several of the performers were barefoot, it was lucky the weather was dry! Each House represented a different Guild of medieval craftsmen and enacted one play in the Cycle, linked by God and His Angels. A hidden choir sang sweetly, Fallen Angels were engulfed by the gaping Mouth of Hell, small Devils danced expressively, there was a magnificent Noah's Ark, and the Cycle ended with tumblers from Moore accompanying the last two Guilds as they made their way down the Field.

Autumn term 1976 and Miss Challis looked forward to her retirement. Queen Anne's was in good heart. She saw little to change her first impression of the School 19 years before: '... a Christian community where every individual mattered, and where laughter and a sense of purpose went hand in hand'. The sense of purpose was stronger than ever. The present generation of girls were well aware that they had more opportunities than ever before, to go on to university and further education, to follow careers the scope of which had been detailed in lectures and talks, in school, by Old Girls, at other colleges

38. Mystery plays.

and other schools. Laughter has always been in plentiful supply at Queen Anne's; its reputation as a happy school had only been enhanced under its fourth Headmistress.

The year rushed on with all the activities which had become traditional under Miss Challis: experiments in Chapel, this year trying the Junior Special Choral and Lower Fifth Singers returning to sit with their forms or Houses to make sure that everyone joined in the singing; involvement with local causes, both seniors and juniors visiting the elderly in Caversham, 75 of whom were entertained to a party in the Hall; fund-raising for a national charity, this year Guide Dogs for the Blind—many ingenious ideas including guessing the weight of Webbe's pet rabbit; the Arts Festival, this year with a medieval theme; juniors did brass-rubbing with Miss Challis in the drawing-room; Activities—people were learning the Charleston, they fenced, did judo, cooked; Excursions—the Latin A level group went to Silchester, and saw the Mildenhall Treasure at the British Museum, the Upper Sixth geographers heard a lecture by Major Blashford-Snell about Stanley, the Lower Sixth politics and economics class went to Reading Crown Court and heard six cases, including one where a grandfather had held up a petrol station with his grandson's toy pistol, the Geography A level group went to Wales and measured beach profiles and stream velocities; in Games, the First XII won at Merton and the Under Fifteen XII drew with another school for the Bentley Salver. It was indeed a happy and busy School that Miss Challis was leaving.

She herself acknowledged the enormous part played by her staff in helping to propel Queen Anne's into a changing world. There were the Housemistresses who were prominent, and known by the whole School, but there were also the 'backroom' people like Miss

Carter who coped with all sorts of domestic problems, from temperamental cooks to tearful charladies, all of whom she treated as part of her extended family. Her excellent sense of humour kept her sane in what could easily have become chaos. But outstanding among the 'backroom' people was Miss Reddall, the School secretary. Self-effacing to the point of invisibility, not many of the School knew of her ability to quote anything at will, nor her ability to draw anything, speedily and accurately. Miss Challis persuaded her to become Boulte's Housemistress, where she was most effective and much-loved, and she continued to be a most excellent secretary. She never put herself forward, but quietly dealt with anything that came her way. Always the first to volunteer, she always put herself last. It was people like Miss Reddall who were at the very core of Queen Anne's and made it the place it was.

2 July 1977 was Miss Challis' last Speech Day and Dr. Muriel Hall, Chairman of the Queen Anne's Committee of Governors, paid tribute to her. She spoke of her outstanding leadership, the high standards she had set, her determination that every one of her girls should achieve the very best in whatever field was hers, be it academic, games, music, acting, painting, while never forgetting the value of service to others. Miss Challis herself had unstintingly made herself available to help others, not only in the broader scope of independent education, but to each and every individual associated with Queen Anne's. Mrs. Blair then spoke of her skill in combining a maximum of individual freedom and happiness with the discipline necessary for a viable community. She had integrated what was valuable in the new freedoms of contemporary ideas and manners with what is fundamental in our Christian standards of excellence in education. Then Mrs. Sharpe ('Cesca Blyth) mother of three Old Girls, and of the then Head Girl, Charlotte Sharpe (Obolensky), presented Miss Challis with a gold watch on behalf of past and present parents. Finally Mrs. Porter, the Second Mistress, unveiled Miss Challis' portrait by William Dring R.A. to a murmur of appreciation from the whole audience. She spoke of Miss Challis' material achievements, the Elliot Wing, the Senior Houses, the improved swimming pool, the Art and Craft building, new classrooms in the quadrangle, new Staff accommodation, the squash court and new tennis courts. But splendid those these were, it was the knowledge that Miss Challis had been Queen Anne's and Queen Anne's had been Miss Challis that was really important.

In her speech, Miss Challis was able to tell her audience that her future life lay in Cheltenham and that she was looking forward to having time to do many things, which made a formidable list: studying local history, listening to modern music, going further with mathematics, pursuing her interest in early civilisations, to find out more about the history of costume as illustrated by monuments in old churches, to learn various types of lettering, investigate Christopher Marlowe, do more dressmaking and embroidery, relate geography with the landscape, to type, learn about old silver, to read all the books she had always wanted to read, and most of all, not to be useless to other people. This was typical of her. To stretch oneself to the uttermost, to pull out the goodliest plums in life's pie, extract what was most worthwhile, but always in the end to be of service to others, this was at the heart of her philosophy for the School.

Chapter VI

The Fifth Headmistress
Miss Scott (1977-1993)

Miss Scott took up her appointment at Queen Anne's School in September 1977, and brought with her a wealth of experience acquired in England and abroad. She was educated at Slough High School, then went on to read French and Italian at Reading University. Her course included a year at Grenoble University, unusual for that time, and her extra-curricular activities indicate some of her later passions at Queen Anne's: choir singer, Captain of Reading University women's athletics team and a member of the Inter Varsity team.

39.   Miss Scott in the study with Nellie, her Cavalier King Charles spaniel.

Her career followed a speedy progression through school hierarchy: she left King Edward's, Witley, after ten years, as Head of Modern Languages and Senior Housemistress, became Deputy Headmistress, then Headmistress, of Limuru Girls' School in Kenya, and was Headmistress of Westwood House School, Peterborough, from 1973 until she came to QAS. Straight girls' boarding must have seemed plain sailing after co-education, mixed day boarding and the multi-racial, multi-lingual, multi-tribal mix that was Limuru.

Miss Scott had applied for the post of Headmistress at the very last moment, but the links with Westminster, the school motto 'Quietness and Strength' and the drawing room as the hub of the School had immediate appeal. The governing body had no hesitation in offering Miss Scott the position, nor she in accepting it.

Her initial perceptions of QAS were of a school and head held in high esteem by the academic community. She soon realised that she would be filling not only the gap left by Miss Challis, but would also have to make up for Miss Reddall, for many years the school secretary and later also Housemistress of Boulte. Their partnership of formidable intellect and genuine warmth would prove a hard act to follow.

Miss Scott wrote in the foreword of her first Chronicle, when she had been at school only a few weeks, of being 'deeply conscious of the privilege that is mine in taking over so goodly a heritage', and of the warmth of the welcome extended to her by everyone connected with the school. Contrary to the experience apparently common amongst new heads, she was delighted with the calibre of the staff she inherited, and had no desire whatsoever to pension off any of them: indeed it is a tribute to them and to her that so many of the 'Old Guard' stayed until their retirement fell due.

It became clear to Miss Scott early on in her time that there was a need to re-examine the standards and general fabric of the school buildings. The first object of her attentions was the kitchens—both main school and Maddock and Ffyler, which both underwent a substantial refit, and some of whose contents were worthy of inclusion in a museum collection!

At this point Maddock and Ffyler lost their gastronomic superiority as menus were standardised throughout the school, but some favourite traditions like 'gypsy tart' were introduced down the field. When Mrs Gardner, the cook in School House, retired in 1987, QAS flirted with outside caterers. Although this experiment was not ultimately a success, the catering firm pioneered cafeteria-style eating and a healthier, tastier choice of things to eat, continued by Mr Faulkner to general acclaim.

A second early priority was to give the Lower VI additional status in recognition of their rôle in running the houses. The Lower VI Form Centre, built next to the Art Block in the Quad, was opened in 1978 and was used as their meeting place during the school day, and as a venue for social events in the evenings. It hosted the VI form talks on Friday evenings, and was used for dinner parties, at which unsuspecting gourmets from neighbouring boys' schools were practised upon by aspiring Cordon-Bleus! Its properly equipped kitchen was a vast improvement on making toast before gas fires in Lower VI sitts or studies, and meant that the novelty of making fudge for entire Saturday afternoons had worn off by the time Michell was reached!

Miss Scott's long term priorities for QAS were a mix of the practical and the ideological. Firstly she was determined to maintain and extend QAS's reputation for games,

40. 'The Old Guard'. Standing, left to right: Mrs. Harding, Miss Ascher, Mrs. Horne, Miss Kirkpatrick, Mrs. Bidder, Mrs. Reid, Mr. Smith, Miss Smith, Miss Driver. Seated, left to right: Miss Bickford, Miss Leahy, Miss Jones, Miss Wollison, Mrs. Smith, Miss Hazel, Mrs. Thomas, Mrs. Audland.

to develop and strengthen its musical life, and to maintain its academic record. Less tangibly her aim was to empower every girl passing through the school to take full advantage of the far greater range of career opportunities available to a woman by developing her individual talent. All this, however, was not to be achieved at the cost of losing the character of QAS as so many generations have known it: the sense of community and support between girls, between girls and staff and among the staff themselves, the importance of helping those less fortunate; the use of creative leisure and the ability to devise their own amusements and to find joy and satisfaction in simple things, all within a Christian framework. This guiding principle, of exposing every girl to as wide a sample of educational and cultural experience as possible, has shaped many of the changes Miss Scott has wrought at QAS in the last 16 years.

The national scene when Miss Scott attained her headship was one of almost unrelieved gloom. Four or so years of inflation, and rumbling industrial unrest, which occasionally erupted into disruptive action, had worn down the morale and financial security of many, who were also increasingly suspicious of Labour's education policy.

In her farewell address to Miss Challis in July 1977, Dr Muriel Hall, the Chairman of the Governors, said that in a time of educational turmoil, 'a school like QAS with its clear sense of purpose and its high standards in all its activities was particularly valued. But at the same time, when more parents than ever would like to send their children to independent

41.   Lower Sixth in evening dress.

schools, inflation was pushing up the cost of running schools, and pushing down, in real terms, parental incomes.'

Miss Scott remained positive and imaginative in the face of changes in education. She was well aware of the demand for good day education in a commuter town like Reading, and felt that QAS could offer the unique advantages of the extended day. Moreover the closer links fostered between the school and local community would surely benefit both parties. The day boarders arrived in 1979, and integrated well. Their school day was identical to a boarder's and their week ended at Saturday lunch time. Webbe became their own house in 1980 and a new separate dining room was created for Wilkins. In the same year a splendid gallery was built in the Chapel to accommodate the Special Choral enabling them to sit together and to lead the singing under the watchful eye of a conductor, as numbers within school had risen from about three hundred and twenty-five to nearer four hundred girls.

Constructive use of time outside the school day also came under the microscope early on. The Arts Festival—of blessed memory!—was not merely retained, but expanded to include first a public speaking element, then many different artistic skills such as dance, photography and creative writing, and also domestic accomplishments such as flower arranging and cookery. Each girl, except those in the Upper VI or Lower VI, was also expected to join one of the clubs which ranged from cookery to chess. Early on an inter-house general knowledge competition was held to increase girls' knowledge of current affairs (and to spend free time more profitably than might otherwise have been the case!).

VI form lectures related to current topics as well as to A level studies were introduced in 1978, and also the opportunity to enter once more for the Duke of Edinburgh's Award Scheme.

The tradition of taking Moores on informal outings to local places of historical interest, as well as the odd theme park, started at this time as a way of ensuring that those girls not familiar with Reading and its surrounds should at least absorb something about the neighbourhood. Littlecote, Windsor Safari Park, Thorpe Park and even, thanks to the good offices of the Clerk and Receiver in London, Mr Hatton, the Lord Mayor's Show became as much a part of a first year at QAS as greasing a lacrosse stick.

Miss Scott did not neglect the more sportingly inclined: two more squash courts were built between 1979 and 1981, and the school participated in outside squash matches for the first time.

On the academic side, Miss Scott brought in the VI form tutorial system. Each new Lower VI former was allocated a tutor to advise her on study skills, help her over the transition to A level work and to discuss her university options. The importance of learning how to study as a foundation for A levels, undergraduate work and beyond was reinforced by a compulsory study skills course throughout the school. The careers' information provision was greatly expanded and girls began to make full use of the two full time careers' teachers now employed.

Miss Scott's first two to three years were ones of consolidation and building on the excellent amenities and traditions QAS already had, before embarking on major new capital projects later in the decade. The new buildings and remarkable improvements to old ones were fairly divided between the competing demands of academic, extra-curricular and comfort!

In 1981 the Elliot Wing was extended to provide a librarian's room, two VI form seminar rooms and a science coaching room, and two of its laboratories were refurbished, as Miss Scott and the science staff were keen to build up science provision at QAS. The remaining laboratories were refurbished in 1985.

Holmes, for years a second Upper VI house, played box and cox with the Sanatorium, but both were completely renovated and found resting places in Derby Road and Henley Road (formerly Camden) respectively in 1983. The cloakroom next to the music cotts, formerly used by Wilkins, became a music room to be used for rehearsals and concerts for small informal groups of musicians. The art block also enjoyed a face-lift at about the same time, and the craft room was renamed the 3D-room, and used for wider applications than tie-dying and making unrecognisable clay figures.

1986 really marked the start of the most noticeable changes to the fabric of QAS. The new entrance, complete with splendid wrought iron gates bearing the crest, and a much safer one-way system, was 'at long last worthy of Queen Anne's', and provided an imposing first glimpse of the school beyond.

Nine years earlier, new safety regulations had decreed that the old swimming pool could no longer be used for diving, so synchronised movements had been introduced and greater emphasis placed on proficiency in personal survival. The opportunity was taken in the interval to re-examine exactly what swimming facilities QAS most needed, and, after much debate and careful planning, a new 'Timberlog' covered, all-year-round, teaching pool was designed for the same site as the old swimmer near Ffyler. The wonderfully airy new building incorporated far better changing facilities, showers, a drying room, and a tea room—unheard of luxury to many Old Girls who provided the furniture for the splendid patio which surrounds it.

It was ready for use in February 1987 and was officially opened by Helen Elkington just after the Easter holidays. This was indeed, as Dr Hall said 'the realisation of a dream'. Pay-off was immediate: in the first summer of its use QAS teams won eight out of eleven matches, and an unexpected bonus was the resurfacing of Harlech tennis courts after a careless, but fortunately well-insured, crane driver had done his worst. The swimming pool has been in constant use ever since and, as well as improving general proficiency in the water, provides an alternative form of exercise for reluctant lacrosse players.

In the same year a new Bursary was built in the copse between the art block and Wilkins gate. The art block continued to be the focus of attention in the next year when it acquired a second storey. The new rooms were used for teaching History of Art which was becoming increasingly popular as an A level subject, and for Art exhibitions. The Bursar's former office became a History of Art library.

It is good to see, amongst the flurry of provision for other people and interests, that the Headmistress herself was not neglected. In 1989 the school bought a detached house at 2b Derby Road, adjoining school property, for Miss Scott to live in, away from much of the term-time hurly-burly. She derived enormous pleasure from both house and garden in her last four years at QAS.

Holmes, the Upper VI overflow at 2a Derby Road, had long been thought unsatisfactory because of the extra supervision required and its decidedly rickety top floor access. Planning permission to extend Michell, so that the whole Upper VI could be housed under one roof, was obtained in 1990.

The splendid new wing took less than six months to build and was opened for use in September 1991. Michell is a striking building and extreme care was taken to integrate the new with the original. All Upper VI now had the same high standard of accommodation and study space. Communication and harmony within the Upper VI in the running of the school were more easily achieved than in the uneasy 'us and them' of the previous two sites.

The main building project of the decade was the new Senior library. This elegant building rises from the old orchard, but happily some of the trees and the 'banger' have been preserved. The school and governors were delighted to name the building after Dr Hall, Ph.D D.Sc., who had served on the Governing Council for over forty years and was its Chairman for 21 of those years. As well as magnificent new accommodation for the books and VI form, the two-storey library comprised a seminar room, archive room, furnished with antiques and with some school artefacts on permanent display, also a librarian's room, as there was a full-time librarian on the staff.

The library was officially opened amid great ceremony by Humphrey Carpenter on 11 January 1990. While the finishing touches were being completed, the former library in the Elliot wing was converted to a lecture theatre with raked seating—a most useful addition to school facilities.

40.   The Muriel Hall library—the opening, Miss Asher and Mrs. Hilliard.

Modern languages acquired a new home with the opening of the Challis Building, a purpose-built block of Language laboratories, classrooms and seminar rooms next to the Elliot Wing. The new facilities enabled the school to offer evening classes in German, Spanish, Italian and Russian, and the building was opened by Mrs Olive Sayce MA, an Oxford modern languages don and long-serving member of the Governing Council, and formally named the Challis Building in honour of Miss M. J. Challis, on Speech Day, 6 July 1992. It was a particular delight that Miss Challis could attend the ceremony. As well as the latest language teaching equipment, the building boasts a satellite dish for receiving European television programmes, a kind gift from its namesake.

One of Miss Scott's talents was to run a tight ship but then to ask for substantial amounts of funding for ventures she passionately believed in. The cases she brought to the Governing Council often bore fruit either from Royal Foundation reserves, or, in the case of the swimming pool and library, in the form of long-term accumulated funds, repayable to the Foundation.

The new Information Technology room, now in the Sykes room, stands as testimony to her foresight within school. The room houses 22 Apple Mac computers, generally agreed to be the most 'user-friendly' and versatile on the market with the merit of compatability with the school's existing hardware and software. Girls can now enjoy specific lessons developing their knowledge of concepts and equipment as well as doing work for other subjects in preparation times.

As well as showpieces of which QAS is justly proud, much work went into improving the general level of comfort in boarding accommodation. Gone were many of the cold, splintery dormitory floors, Ffyler 'pooh cupboards' and housemaids' pantries, and in their place, carpets and washing cubicles. Moore, Maddock and Ffyler also had new boilers, which made running out of hot water—most dreaded of all domestic eventualities—a thing of the past. Washing machines and driers make a better job of laundry than trying to clean muddy games kit in the bath ...

The Housemistresses' accommodation in Ffyler and Wilkins was enlarged and made self-contained to enable married couples to live there, and staff accommodation in general made more comfortable and attractive. Few of the form rooms escaped the carpet-layers' attentions.

These improvements to the general standard of living, as well as the culinary revolution wrought by Mr Faulkner, meant that life at QAS in the nineties scales heights of hedonism which would be scarcely credible to earlier generations cracking the ice in their wash bowls on winter mornings!

The casual observer, contemplating the new buildings and improvements to existing ones which happened during Miss Scott's time, could be forgiven for thinking that therein lay the greatest shake-up to QAS in this era. But bubbling under the flow of everyday activities was a period of considerable educational and social changes.

The most significant educational change came in 1988 with the first GCSE examinations which replaced the former GCEs and CSEs. The old system of regurgitating facts, figures and diagrams had long been considered (in some educational circles) to be unfair to any but the brightest pupils, and the new system aimed to provide the opportunity for all candidates to show what they knew, understood and could do. Course-work would be assessed and would form between twenty and forty per cent of final marks. A change in the emphasis in different subjects was welcomed by many departments—the English department for example was pleased that a pupil's genuine, personal response to her reading, and her skills of listening and speaking would be counted. Taking the syllabus away from pure theory and closer to 'real life' was the aim behind the new science courses, as well as addressing current social, economic and environmental issues. The understanding of ideas and their application was now required rather than the reproduction of specific examples illustrating those ideas. However, the very fact that the new examination grades all levels of attainment has laid it open to charges of lacking academic rigour.

In the same year the Education Reform Act was passed, the most significant piece of education law since the 1944 Education Act. The bulk of its content concerned the National Curriculum, now compulsory in all state schools, but not yet in the independent sector. The National Curriculum merits mentioning here, as it embodies the same change in emphasis to practical skills of problem-solving and application as the GCSE examination, and attempts to treat subjects across the whole curriculum, rather than confining them rigidly to their traditional disciplines.

Laudable though these changes may be, the continuing complaint in both state and independent sectors has been the speed of change and resultant inadequate preparation. As Miss Scott summed it up on Speech Day 1992, 'It really seems quite unbelievable that, whereas in the past major changes in examination formats took place at two, three or even four decade intervals, this time two major changes have taken place within the secondary schooling of one child. Those of us who began our teaching days in the fifties have at least heard of School Certificate and Matriculation, yet it really is quite extraordinary that the young and old of today have to learn a new educational vocabulary almost every year. The effect of all this upon staff training has been quite devastating.'

Long before the GCSE and the National Curriculum appeared on the Statute Book, Miss Scott had started to broaden and update the subjects on offer at QAS, for example by introducing computing. Miss Scott always professed herself to be very much against excessive specialisation too early, and she extended the range of courses outside A level work available to the VI form. Girls could choose whether or not to take formal qualifications in their extra subjects or to do them for fun. Her firm belief in the importance of a flexible approach to modern life led her to bring in a new General Course for the Lower VI, where girls could study art, music, European literature, politics, philosophy and economics as well as the influence of technology on our age. These fortunate beings were encouraged to delve into whatever areas particularly fascinate them. Latterly, the teaching and resources for this course were shared with local schools, so the social element became an added interest.

In 1987, AS levels were introduced. Either taken after a year of full-time study or after two years of part-time study, these were intended to be half an A level. The aim was to broaden the VI form curriculum and to combine arts and sciences, with a view to bringing our final qualifications closer to those in Europe, where school leavers have studied a wider range of subjects. Over the years the range of subjects available at A level was extended to include economics, history of art, classical civilisation and general studies.

Two years after her arrival Miss Scott brought a new element into the Arts Festival, which went on to gather such momentum that a Queen Anne's girl, Catharine Peppiatt, won the prize for the Best British Speaker in the first ever World Debating Championships in 1988 and was placed sixth overall. Encouraged initially by Mrs Smith and continued by Mrs Simpson and Mrs Cook, public speaking became a pillar of extra-curricular life, and skills were hotly contested at the annual inter-house competition, run at senior and junior levels. Miss Scott's belief in the importance of being able to put oneself across powerfully in words stemmed from a belief in female assertiveness: in order to get on in the world girls had to be as good if not better than the boys—and be noticed! As the first woman ever to read the Epistle in Peterborough Cathedral and one who has preached in Westminster Abbey, she could be said to live by her precepts ...

The interest in drama was always characteristic of the school, and continued to derive further impetus from Miss Scott's emphasis on the importance of the spoken word. A school play—*Twelfth Night*—was performed for the first time for a few years in 1979. It met with 'rave reviews', not only from the school, but from parents as well. Since then, House plays, Arts Festival entries and 'Bust-Up' entertainments too numerous to mention were performed, and drama became a GCSE option in 1989. The School play became a firm fixture on the calendar and works as varied as Marlowe's *Faustus* and *Daisy Pulls It Off* were ably produced by Miss Bickford, Mrs Mees, Miss Asher and Mr Garner with Mrs Cowling putting her considerable talents to work on the costumes and make-up. The standards reached by individuals were high enough to win plaudits in open competition: in 1990, two girls, Belinda Berkeley and Alison Morrow, were placed second in the entire country for their duologue from *Twelfth Night* (clearly a lucky play for QAS) in the 'Shakespeare on the platform' competition. Interestingly, one of the judges was an Old Girl, Margaret Wolfit, 1943-46 (now Mrs Oates), who was quite overcome that her old school should have done so well.

The limitations of the hall as a venue for dramatic and musical productions have been apparent for some time, and innovative use has been made on occasion of the Chapel for live performance. *Dawn on Our Darkness*, by Richard Tydeman, and a memorable performance of Eliot's *Murder in the Cathedral* were staged there. As a fitting commemoration of the school's centenary, a Performing Arts Centre has been built to adjoin Michell in Derby Road. Its primary function is as a concert venue, although it will certainly be used to stage drama productions without the restriction of the proscenium arch. As well as providing an appropriate setting for the wealth of musical and dramatic talent at QAS, it gives girls more experience in the technical management of productions such as lighting, stage and set changing.

Many a girl discovered the delights of part-singing, Church music or playing in an orchestra at Queen Anne's, and it is probably true that never has more musical activity been built into the timetable. Miss Scott's strong desire to enhance the school's already good reputation for music led to all sorts of innovations. All girls learnt music in the classroom for the first three years, so that they could read music and have a chance to try out different instruments. Alongside the Junior and Senior orchestras a variety of smaller instrumental ensembles sprang up which performed publicly on occasion, but often just for fun. Aspiring rock stars tried out their ideas on synthesisers and electric guitars, not to mention timpani which could be heard from miles away!

The strong tradition of singing encompassed the Junior and Senior choirs, Special Choral, and a Choral Society as well as smaller, less formal groups. Everyone, not merely the very best, was encouraged to perform and the less formal 'listen and play' concerts were generally well attended. Queen Anne's continued to join other schools for combined choral works and musicals, such as *The Pirates of Penzance*, *The Sorcerer* and *La Belle Hélène* all with Reading School. In 1991, the lower school performed Britten's *Noye's Fludde*, a musical and technical feat requiring the ability to sing, act and build an ark simultaneously. The production's undoubted success was a tribute to the musical and technical talents of the producers, Mr. Howell and Mr. Garner. Somehow, word reached the B.B.C. and 'the next thing we knew there was request for the cast to perform a little of the 'Fludde' for television'. Any dreams of stardom lurking in the actresses' hearts were rudely shattered by the freezing, boring realities of filming!

Surely the highlight of any musician's career at QAS would be to have gone on tour with the choir, as they have now done on three occasions. The first trip in 1986 was to Germany and Austria, and, as Jacqueline Singer wrote, 'the one question bothering us was whether or not the Germans and Austrians would be at all interested in hearing an English choir give a concert, when they must have their own institutions in abundance. It was therefore extremely gratifying to find such a warm welcome wherever we went'.

The second tour, two years later, visited the cradle of the Renaissance; Venice, Padua, Sienna and Florence. Yet again the choir received a rapturous reception everywhere they went, and their thorough preparation and muscical skill meant they triumphed over two unplayable organs and Italian informality—wandering about during concerts, not knowing which parts of the service the visiting choir was to sing and so on. Seeing the baptismal entry for Vivaldi dated 1678 in Bragora was a compensating thrill.

In 1990 at the suggestion of Canon Colin Semper, by now a School Governor, the choir went to Eastern Europe for the first time, to Hungary. They were honoured to perform a concert in St Stephen's Basilica in Esztergom, Hungary's largest church and centre of Roman Catholicism since the 13th century. They used this and a fixture in Budapest where they sand Kodaly's 'Ave Maria' at the altar rail in view of the audience, to hone their skills for the fourteenth international Bela Bartok choir competition to be held in Debreçen, on Hungary's eastern edges. 'Queen Anne's, Iskola Leanykara, Caversham, Nagy Britania' was proud to be the sole representative of its country, and acquitted itself very creditably during the four days of the competition. The Hungarians awarded them the ultimate accolade of the slow hand-clap once they realised that two songs were sung in their native tongue. This tour was particularly memorable for the participants because they experienced at first hand a Europe 40 years behind our own, taking its first stumbling steps to freedom and blinking in the sunlight.

Miss Brewitt-Taylor, who led all the tours, gave voice to the feelings of many. 'We were touched and humbled by the warmth of our reception everywhere, impressed by the dedication of the Hungarian choirs, shocked by the plight of Rumanian choirs who cannot buy the Church music they want to sing now that the new religious freedom permits. I gave my tattered copy of Schubert's Psalm 23 to a Ukrainian who attended our concert in Debreçen. He was quite overcome with emotion'.

In July 1993, the choir followed the example of the lacrosse teams by venturing across the Atlantic to the east coast of the U.S.A. They sang at two Eucharists in New York and Connecticut and gave several more concerts, including an unaccompanied recital at

43.   The choir in the Chapel and taking part in the Music Festival at Debreçen, Hungary.

Washington National Cathedral. Their performances were greeted with as much warmth and enthusiasm as they had been in Europe, and the girls were lavishly entertained. A visit to Tanglewood for a concert on the lawn proved a memorable highlight of the tour.

Nearer home, the choir continued well-loved traditions such as the Advent Carol Service at St Peter's, Caversham, and over the years it has been invited to sing evensong at some of the most ancient and prestigious cathedrals, including Winchester, Wells, Salisbury and Chichester. Other invitations to small venues have a special significance for Queen Anne's, such as Felpham in Sussex, the retirement home of the Rev. Neville and Mrs. Joan Smith, who taught at QAS for 18 years. Miss Scott has been keen to further QAS links with Westminster, and in 1980 the school had its own service in the Abbey, 'not to celebrate any particular milestone in our history, but simply to rejoice in our connection with Westminster'. On the occasion of its 90th birthday in 1984, the school presented itself with robes for the choir, which were worn for the first time at the celebratory service in Westminster Abbey.

Promising musicians have been fortunate enough to attend the occasional master class given by eminent performers. As most musicians start with the piano, it made sense to focus on this instrument, and Christopher Elton, Michael Young and Geoffrey Buckley have all shared their expertise with the school. Jeanette Masocchi has given a vocal master class. The lucky few who attended these sessions found them to provide stimulating new insight.

Running parallel to Miss Scott's wish to bring music to the forefront of school activities was an equally strong desire to continue QAS' tradition of success on the sports field. In 1982 the U15 XII were unbeaten in all school matches, and won their day at Merton which made QAS the only school to pull off the 'double'. On Championship Day the first XII came third. In 1984 the first XII became National Schools' Champions, beating all the other finalists at Merton, to bear home the National Westminster Shield in triumph. This was but the start of a remarkable run of success—they were champions six times and runners-up thrice.

Their prowess was rewarded by the first ever overseas lacrosse tour to Canada and New England, in the spring of 1985. The tour started in Toronto, where the team were hosted by Havergal College. As well as playing their first match, the team saw the highlights of Toronto, the CN tower and Ontario Science Centre, and Niagara Falls. Four days later they flew to Boston, where they visited historic sites of the War of Independence—with commentary from the other side's perspective! This first tour was an undoubted success, and a tremendous credit to the participants and organisers, Miss English (Mrs MacLean) and Miss Logan.

The notable successes of the first XII on English soil were matched by those of the junior teams throughout the period, who regularly came home with trophies from their sections of the major tournaments, the Berkshire and West and Merton. At one point no fewer than seven such trophies graced the display cabinet in the Front Hall.

In 1989 another highly successful tour to the East coast of the United States was arranged starting in New York and finishing in Boston by way of Connecticut and Rhode Island. The team enjoyed a hectic mixture of sight seeing and sport, and experiencing American life at the hands of their generous host families and schools.

44.   One of the many triumphant Merton champion teams, 1991. Back row, left to right: Laura Hopkins,
Deborah Scobie, Nicola Godfrey, Annabel Blagg, Fiona Piper; middle row: Belinda Berkeley, Janice Tsang,
Cinzia Francis-Marletta, Emily Boyd; front row: Charlotte Starmer-Smith, Sarah Taylor, Jenny Colston-
Reeves (Vice-Capt.), Joanna Whitty (Capt.), Lena Kirton, Charlotte Lawson-Smith, Melissa Weatherill. Under-
15 tennis: Melissa Weatherill, Deborah Scobie, Charlotte McMullen, Alexandra Skinner. Steven Redgrave is
pictured naming the *Pilgrim*.

In the same year Downe House hosted an invitation tournament for the first time. The first XII came home with the senior trophy, but the U15 gallantly conceded theirs to their hosts. A year later, QAS invited six of the best lacrosse schools to its own tournament and these invitation tournaments became a firm fixture on the lacrosse calendar.

As well as bringing its own name to prominence, QAS players were also regularly selected for the Berkshire and Junior West teams. In 1990 the West won the Territorial tournament for the first time in 11 years, aided by four QAS players, and in 1992, no fewer than 17 played for Berkshire. Three Junior West players were nominated for Junior England trials. Girls have also had their share of responsibility—Sarah Ram captained the Junior West team in 1982 and Camilla Peppiatt in 1985, as well as being Vice Captain of the Junior England team.

In July 1992 the first XII ventured to the Antipodes. This adventure had necessarily to be preceded by some serious fund-raising, and to that end, a Parents' Committee convened to produce a glossy brochure. Letters of support from Virginia Wade and David Gower incited parents, governors and lacrosse enthusiasts to acts of generosity, so the dream could become reality.

When Miss Scott arrived at QAS, tennis had been going through a disappointing phase, but in 1983 eight existing courts were converted to all-weather surfaces so, weather permitting, tennis could be played all year round. The resulting improvement meant the first VI going through to the regional finals of the Aberdare Cup. Enthusiasm also grew: in 1987, 180 girls entered the singles championships, that is nearly half the school! At this point QAS entered another tournament for the first time, the Midland Bank Winter League, where it played consistently well, winning the Southern region in 1990. That year saw the zenith of recent achievements on the tennis courts as two QAS girls, Melissa Weatherill and Deborah Scobie, won the U15 Harpenden School girls' tennis tournament—the first QAS girls to do so since 1955—and Lucy Goodall the U15 Berkshire Schoolgirls' singles championship.

Swimming was until recently a similarly brief interlude in the school's calendar. The breakthrough came in 1987 with the opening of the magnificent new indoor pool, when there was a notable improvement and QAS won nine out of eleven matches. Swimming continued to gather momentum, so that in 1990 QAS took the competition head on, and hosted its first invitation swimming gala.

Since then QAS has had enough confidence in its ability to enter the National final of the School Team Championships, and the Berkshire School Relay. In 1992 four new records were established at the English Schools' Relay Championships.

Girls in the VI form has long enjoyed a wider range of games and sports than their juniors, but gradually more choice became available throughout the school. In 1980 a trampoline was bought, and its popularity necessitated the forming of a weekly club where girls could work towards proficiency awards.

Two years later, rowing was reintroduced under the keen eye of a Queen Anne's father, Wing Commander J. S. Pilgrim-Morris. To their credit the first ever coxed four came eighth out of fifteen in the Women's Novice Section at Henley Fours Head that year. The oarswomen also enjoyed making up mixed crews with rowing schools nearby and diversifying into eights and sculling. Their hard work was rewarded in 1987 when the coxed four won the Reading Schools' Head of the River race; so much interest was generated that the school bought its own boat, and in February 1993 launched a brand new modern one, named Pilgrim, after the Wing-Commander.

Gymnastics also enjoyed something of a revival in the last ten years, initiated by the change from Modern Educational to Olympic. The inter-house gymnastics competition became a firm fixture in the school's calendar.

Athletics began to play a more important part in the summer term. As well as the inter-house competition QAS now competed with other schools and held the first full Sports Day for a long time in 1992. Two girls represented Reading at Inter-District level. The Pentathlon event was also contested in the summer, at both Senior and Junior levels, with trophies donated by Miss Scott.

Older OGs may note with amusement that cricket was re-introduced in 1989, by Mr. Garner, Classics Master, drama producer and erstwhile cricketer, and that two teams were invited to a six-a-side tournament at Eton no less .... Although they were far from disgracing themselves, they had some way to go before venturing to the hallowed sward of the Oval! The resounding refrain stressed what fun it was, and in particular that interested players from the IVs to the VI played together.

The newest sport on offer at QAS was sailing, available only to the VI form, who have even ventured into competition at the Berkshire Schools' Sailing Centre on the gravel pits at Theale.

Theatre visits and scientific field trips had long been a part of school life, but now art historians have been to Italy and Holland, junior linguists to France in term-time, 'et in Arcadia the LVI classicists'. As much as undoubtedly enhancing the subject, the girls had some priceless encounters with their host countries such as 'being forced to eat barbecued pigs' hearts, while smiling and trying not to burst into tears'.

In 1990 Queen Anne's participated in a group exchange with Le Caousou school in Toulouse for the first time. The advantage of supervision was that younger girls can take part, and the exposure to French language and culture in the second year gave young linguists far greater confidence and enthusiasm.

One annual trip was purely for fun, namely the ski trip. Long suffering members of staff led recently by the Head of Mathematics, Mr. Rowell, chaperoned generations through the pitfalls (literally) of sprained joints and 'whirlwinds of dangerous Frenchmen', to receive, triumphant at the end of the week, awards for 'Piste Bully' or 'Piste Princess'. Very sensibly all the trips were preceded by lessons on the dry slope at Aldershot so that few nerves or inhibitions lingered.

Much has already been said about the plays and concerts, but the VI form conference deserves a special mention. Since 1980 QAS has hosted an annual conference for the VI forms of eight or so local schools. The subject has always been topical and speakers eminent. After an opening address, VI formers split into smaller discussion groups to focus on a particular area of the subject, then reconvened to put their views in open forum. All the conferences broadened the students' knowledge of the subject and improved their skills of argument and expression, but 1991's conference on Eastern Europe stood out particularly. Seven students came from behind what was the Iron Curtain to give vivid first hand accounts of contemporary life under the uncertain régimes succeeding communism. No doubt they would have been happy to see the 350 children's garments which QAS sent to Rumania in direct response to hearing about conditions there.

The school hosted the second ever World Debating and Public Speaking Championships jointly with Blue Coat School in 1989, where students from seven countries competed. Logistical nightmares aside, it was an enjoyable experience and a chance to make contacts abroad, should any lacrosse players, musicians or art historians be smitten with wanderlust.

QAS then was very much on the map as a venue for a range of academic, sporting and social activities, not only because of the excellence of its facilities, but equally of the foresight and commitment of the Headmistress and staff, who realised that education in its broadest sense could not flourish in a vacuum.

Artefacts, however, flourish well in a vacuum and QAS joined Globelink, the schools' link with the new Globe Theatre in London. In June 1992 Claire Harding and Georgina Palmer buried a time capsule in the foundations of the building in return for a £200 donation to the fund. The capsule contains material from the 17th, 19th and 20th centuries, commemorating the founding of Grey Coat and Queen Anne's, and from the schools in 1992. The opening ceremony of the New Globe at which the burial took place was attended by HRH Prince Edward, and the crew of 'Newsround', who gave Georgina her first TV interview!

One could be forgiven for wondering how these girls managed to fit in any work at all, let alone of the standard required to gain the sparkling results to keep up the tradition of excellence established and continued by previous Headmistresses. However, percentage

45.   Some of the House staff on the patio of Miss Scott's new home. Left to right: Miss Moyle (Maddock), Mrs. Jackson (Wisdome), Mrs. Brown (Ffyler), Mrs. Whitaker (Michell), Miss Scott, Mrs. Weir (Moore), Mrs. Hooper (Boulte) and Mrs. Falconer (Michell).

pass rates at GCSE and A level ran very close to 100 per cent, and well over 90 per cent of the UVI went on to University or Polytechnic.

In 1985 Karen Rudgard won an Open Scholarship to read Classics at St John's College, Oxford, the last year in which such awards were given, and in 1992 Lena Thia was awarded a scholarship in medicine after completing her first year at Liverpool.

QAS also has its share of OGs pre-eminent in academic and public life. To name but a few: Jean Bannister, Fellow of Somerville College, Oxford, Lesley Abdela M.P., Frances Heaton (née Whidborne), Head of the Takeover Panel, Posy Simmonds cartoonist, Celia Haddon columnist and author, Jenny Seagrove actress and Anna Harvey (née Folkard) deputy editor of British Vogue.

Miss Scott always kept in the foreforont of her mind the need for continuing excellence in the school's achievements and for first class facilities, in order to meet the changing expectations of pupils and parents, present and future. It was not enough, however, to rely on indirect publicity to ensure that QAS came to the notice of parents considering single-sex education for a daughter, or to the attention of preparatory school heads recommending the next step for their charges.

In 1982, 80 members of the Incorporated Association of Preparatory Schools asked to visit QAS, a request with which Miss Scott was only too happy to comply. The good impression created was furthered by a brand new colour prospectus, to replace the former edition. The prospectus was produced by professionals and does full justice in the text and photographs to what QAS offered. It has since been joined by two 'younger sisters', a VI form prospectus aimed at those joining QAS for their A levels and a first year prospectus, comprising photographs and text provided exclusively from members of Moore House.

A video, for loan to prospective parents, was also made in 1987. Athough undeniably a useful medium for showing off QAS, the first version would now be considered rather old-fashioned, containing as it did the earnestly 'talking heads' of Housemistresses extolling the schools' virtues. The 1990 version focused exclusively on the girls, showing a representative from each age-group, covering both the academic and extra curricular. The video is a useful backdrop at exhibitions.

QAS had also marketed its musical prowess on cassette; on one occasion principally as a permanent record of the 90th birthday celebrations in 1984. In 1986 the School Chronicle was also changed to match the new prospectus in appearance. The larger size made for greater clarity, with more photographs and better reproduction of black and white drawings.

One report quite fascinating in the objectivity of its detail was that provided by the Berkshire Social Services Department, in connection with the Children Act, 1989. The report cannot be quoted except as a whole, but permission has been given to use part of their conclusion which reads 'overall there is a feeling of girls caring for and about each other'.

Since its inception, members of QAS have been conscious of those less fortunate than themselves, and helping them in practical ways or by fund-raising has always been high amongst its priorities. Some of the earlier initiatives may seem quaint now, such as knitting socks for Servicemen, but the same spirit of compassion moved the present generation of girls to set to with their knitting needles and work baskets to construct garments for Rumanian orphans. QAS also perpetuated its long tradition of sending clothes and blankets to those in need by joining the Queen Mary's London Needlework Guild in 1980. It was set up to help find clothes for old and young people in London who could not afford to buy new ones, and QAS now sent the some of the proceeds of the Arts Festival to this excellent cause.

Work in the community continued to occupy the free time of the older girls. For years LV visited old people locally, not just to drink tea and chat, but also to garden and help them to do things they could no longer manage. The annual Christmas party in the hall for local elderly people was still enjoyed by everyone whether a carol singer, handbell ringer, entertainer, purveyor of tea, guest or Father Christmas.

QAS continued to distribute its help widely, by choosing a different charity to support every term. These varied immensely from the well-established famous names like Oxfam and Save the Children to causes less well publicised or closer to home, such as Riding for the Disabled or the Brookfield School for Autistics. Chapel collections were always given to charity, but girls gave unstintingly of their time and ingenuity to raise money in more imaginative ways. The House fêtes and bonfire parties were ever popular, the food stands exerting the greatest pull, as well as sponsored walks, silences (to the incredulity of many members of staff and parents), starvation lunches and mufti days. The amount of money raised was quite astonishing: in the year 1991/92 a total of £7,543.54 was raised, £264.63 of that in four days in response to an emergency appeal for children in Albania.

Two charitable initiatives lasted longer than a term. In 1985, the autumn term charity was the Starehe Boys' School in Kenya, but QAS furthered its commitment by sponsoring one boy, Dickson Achillah, so that he could complete his education. He successfully did so, and during its course, wrote regularly to some of the juniors and even received a visit from a roving VI former.

More recently QAS raised funds to sponsor three of its Old Girls to do voluntary work in their year off under the auspices of the School's Partnership Worldwide. Catherine Hawley and Suzanne Whittaker both spent their year teaching in Nyeri but also had a brief time helping in an orphanage in Nepal, and Eleanor Monbiot taught in Kenya. An added benefit was the preservation of close ties with three leavers.

Miss Scott's views on the Old Girls as an extended family coincide with Miss Holmes': the Society has become more active in recent years with the compilation of a more reliable data base. The revival of the idea of sending certain year groups a specific invitation to get together at the summer meeting has revived interest in the 'old place'—not merely out of sentimentality, but as a useful network of contacts in professional or civic life.

Finally, then, to the goodbyes. In a tenure of 16 years, there are inevitably changes in the staffroom, although it says much for the loyalty of the staff and their dedication to QAS that these were not more numerous. It would be impossible to mention everybody, but the length of time some members of staff spent as QAS is remarkable. Many of us remember with affection the staff who taught us and looked after us in Miss Challis' time, and who continued to support Miss Scott until their retirement. Miss Wollison, the formidable Head of English, Miss Stride, Boulte's equally redoubtable matron, Dr. Hardy and Mrs. Deuters on the medical side all retired in 1980, Miss Stride after 29 years! In the next three years Mrs. Porter, Head of Science for 12 years and latterly Deputy Headmistress, Miss Davis who taught Mathematics and was Housemistress of Webbe for 15 years, Miss Pugh, Maddock's devoted matron for 17 years, Mrs. Hart who taught French for 20 years and later headed the Modern Languages department, all retired. Miss Hatton, teacher of piano and violin and Housemistress of Moore, surprised and delighted everyone by leaving to get married after 32 years at QAS.

In 1987 another wave of long-serving members of staff left the school in the persons of Mrs. Bidder, Michell's Housemistress for 12 years, Mr. Murray, Head of Classics, Mrs. Turton, Mrs. Harding, the kindly admissions secretary and Mrs. Gardner, who did sterling work in the School House kitchens.

1988 marked the nadir of the 'Old Guard's retirement', when Miss Driver, Miss Bickford who taught History for 27 years and who also used her talents producing plays and arranging flowers, Miss Hazel, devoted teacher of keyboard instruments and the violin and Chapel organist for over 20 years, Mrs. Reid who taught Mathematics part-time for 23 years, Miss Smith for 20 years Ffyler's beloved matron, Mrs. Mees, who during her 21 years taught English and History, was Housemistress of Wisdome and ran the school libraries, and Mrs. Hide, vivacious Head of Modern Languages, all left. Between them they had served QAS for a staggering total of one hundred and sixty-one years! The staffroom must have been a very different place in September 1988. The following two years saw the retirement of Mrs. Walling, French teacher for 16 years and Head of Modern Languages for her final one, the Rev. Neville and Mrs. Joan Smith who served the school as Chaplain and teacher of English respectively for 18 years, (Mrs. Smith also taking on Wilkins as Housemistress for her final two years), Mrs. Wiltshire (formerly Miss Hester), Head of Mathematics for 17 years.

In 1992 Group Captain Probyn, the Bursar, and Mrs. Old, his assistant, both retired. They had made an excellent team producing immaculate accounts for 14 years. In the same year Mr. Tim Hatton OBE retired as Clerk and Receiver to the Foundation, and tribute was paid to his calm and expert advice and his wealth of knowledge. Finally, Dr. Hall stepped down as Chairman of the Governing Council in 1992, but her expertise continued to be greatly valued as a Council member.

The debt QAS owes to these devoted people was incalculable, and warm tributes to their service have appeared in the Chronicle. One who should receive special mention—Miss Mary Driver, who spent the whole of her her career at QAS spanning 39 years, and combined the teaching of Classics with her rôle as Housemistress of Ffyler for 25 of those years. She was acknowledged by girls and staff alike as being the best teacher in the school, elucidating the mysteries of Latin and Greek grammar to those not especially good at parsing or construing, and revealing the excitement of the *Iliad* to those who were. She employed her teaching skills to good effect in the house too, teaching all but the most impervious junior to knit. This was typical of her unstinting dedication to her house, where she was much respected, if considered rather formidable by anyone below the LVI! In 1979 she became Deputy Headmistress, but refused to give up her beloved Ffyler, assuming the increased workload without a murmur. Fortunately her responsibilities did not prevent her from writing the most kindly and apposite valedictions in the *Chronicle*, or composing a masterly obituary to William, the school cat: 'dignus est qui Latine laudetur, quod apud magistros Latinas sedere solebat saepius quam apud alios'—('It is fitting that his praises should be sung in Latin, for he was accustomed to spend more time with the Latin teachers than the others ...')—and that undoubtedly because she was a legendary cat lover herself!

Retirements, though sad, are to be expected, as indeed are the subsequent deaths of older members of staff. Staff and girls alike were very sorry, however, that a few past members of staff were deprived of a long and fulfilling retirement by their untimely deaths, namely Miss Stride, Mrs. Porter, Miss Hazel and Mrs. Bidder who all died within a few years of retirement.

Deaths at school are a different matter, and QAS was devastated in 1991 by the tragic death of LVI former, Charlotte Starmer-Smith, then of Mr. Derek Hopkins who taught economics and finally of its beloved Deputy Headmistress, Mrs. Anne Hilliard in 1992. Miss Scott described the year as one in which 'sadnesses seemed to outnumber joys, but, amid the the universal sorrow and disbelief, this painful experience brought out the best in girls, and the spirit of community was, if anything, strengthened'. One thousand daffodil bulbs were planted in Charlotte Starmer-Smith's memory, and, as a perfect memorial to Mrs. Hilliard, a fully automatic weather station was given to the geography department as well as a tree with a seat beside it.

It is beyond question that QAS bears manifest impressions of Miss Scott's 16-year tenure, but it is salutary to see, even with such a strong helmswoman, that the school ran smoothly when that helmswoman was on a study visit to the U.S.A. with a party of other Heads from the United Kingdom. Miss Asher and Mrs. Hilliard were left in charge, and deputised to the letter, even ensuring that Miss Scott would be greeted by the news of another Merton victory on her return!

Their practice at 'holding the fort' was to come in useful again in 1991 when Miss Scott had a sabbatical term, and again in 1992/1993 when Miss Asher became Acting Headmistress during Miss Scott's absence. Having served the school for 16½ years, first as Housemistress of Boulte, after Miss Reddall, then from 1988 as one of the Deputy Headmistresses when Miss Driver retired, Miss Asher had hoped that her last years at QAS would be quiet ones. Instead she needed all the strength she could muster in order to cope, firstly with the sudden death of her devoted colleague and friend, Mrs. Hilliard, then with running the school during Miss Scott's final year, and lastly assisting the new Headmistress, Mrs. Forbes, to take the reins. QAS is most fortunate that she has been willing to extend her service by these vital extra years.

It was Miss Scott's 'sincere prayer that I may be given the strength to lead the school quietly and competently towards its centenary in Caversham in 1994'—and so very cruel that ill health should deprive her of the crowning point of her career. To her immense regret in the autumn of 1992 her doctors advised her and the governors that she should retire a year early in the summer of 1993.

She was heartbroken not to be considered fit enough to lead the school during her last year but the Centenary will be much enhanced by her energetic contribution to its planning, and her Chairmanship of the History Committee. The school was delighted to see her at social and artistic events during her last year, and glad that she helped to prepare the candidates for confirmation in the spring, and took a full part in the service.

The summer of 1993 saw a long series of farewells, beginning with Old Girls' Day in May, when Susie Craig (1972-1978), Miss Scott's first Head Girl, presented her with a cheque and a bouquet of QAS red roses on behalf of the Old Girls' Society.

The School held a special presentation to Miss Scott on the afternoon of Speech Day, 3 July, at which there was a veritable exchange of gifts between Miss Scott and her many well-wishers. The first speaker, Mrs. P. I. Morgan, J.P. (née Tucker 1947-1952), Chairman of the Governing Council, expounded the outstanding qualities of headship which had been clearly apparent in Miss Scott from the outset: her pride in every pupil's achievement, her brilliance with figures and budgeting and her vision for QAS, as well as outlining her many and various achievements and innovations. As a lasting reminder of the school's grateful thanks and recognition of all she had done, she gave Miss Scott a brooch in the form of a golden rose.

It was then Dr. Hall's turn to take the dais in order to present the portrait to the school, on behalf of the trustees and Royal Foundation of Grey Coat Hospital. As she had worked with Miss Scott as Chairman of the Governing Council for all but the last year of her headship, she was best qualified to describe Miss Scott's immense dedication to QAS, her ability to select first-class staff, whose commitment reflected the commitment at the top, and not least her 'tremendous energy which left one feeling somewhat breathless!'

It was a particular pleasure that the artist, Mr. John Walton, Chairman of the Federation of British Artists, could be there to hear the gasps of admiration, which greeted the portrait as it was unveiled by Miss Asher. It would hang as the fifth in the series in the Hall, each of whose subjects had made their individual contribution to the school. Whilst Miss Holmes would doubtless raise an eyebrow or two at much of contemporary life at QAS, she would surely recognise the spirit of service she inaugurated, and the knowledge of and concern for each girl embodied by Miss Scott.

Georgina Palmer, the Head Girl, then presented Miss Scott with a magnificent bouquet of red roses, wooing her listeners with a witty speech, alluding to Nellie and a shared love of Cavalier King Charles Spaniels.

Mr. Barry Weatherill, a parent of 15 years' association with the school and father of the present Games Captain, spoke on behalf of the parents and presented Miss Scott with a camcorder, tripod and operating manual, plus a residual cheque, enough to fund an exotic holiday during which she could practise her newly acquired skills. Mr. Weatherill referred to Miss Scott's foresight in changes affecting the education scene and her enhancing of the school's buildings, music and sport. The school had 'adapted cautiously but appropriately to changing circumstances to create the same product' with which, as a long-standing customer, he could profess himself well satisfied.

The climax of the afternoon was Miss Scott's address. A remarkable total of 2,000 young ladies had passed through her hands, and she had endeavoured to pass on to each of them the importance of learning to value themselves and thus other people, and the ability to live together as a community. She outlined her plans for an active and fulfilling retirement; including travelling to Australia and New Zealand, working in Westminster Abbey and possibly Glyndebourne and studying for a degree in History of Art with the Open University, concluding her moving speech by thanking parents past and present for lending her their lovely daughters during their most interesting, if not their most formative years.

As with the other four headmistresses in the first hundred years at Caversham, QAS would always remain dear to her heart, as well as being the source of her greatest professional pride and achievements.

Epilogue

What of the Future?

We may not be able to look into the future but we must plan for it. The Founders of Grey Coat Hospital were, as we have read, men who paid attention to practical detail but they were also men of vision. They held firm to their purpose. Miss Holmes, too, looking to the welfare of her girls, adapted to changes but her steadfastness to her aims cannot be doubted.

We have a flourishing school today and must thank our predecessors, both for their readiness to face up to changing circumstances and for their ability to see beyond the temporal and the mutable. The way forward also depends upon these two attributes. Education is constantly subject to changes of policy but our staff will continue to ensure that we follow initiatives in response to the evolving demands of society. Whatever adjustments we make, however, to what we teach and the way in which we teach it, we can be guided by the same sense of vision as that which has endured for a hundred years: an appropriate education for the girls in our charge.

None of us can tell what the 21st century holds, nor what Queen Anne's second century will bring, although it is certain that we must look outwards towards Europe and a wider community. The prospects are exciting. Sustaining us through our challenges remains the value which we affirm and share in the chapel each day. In my first week of office I received a letter which said, 'I understand that in years I am the oldest QAS Old Girl (93). I owe so much to Miss Holmes' training, especially the religious upbringing she instilled in us'. Poised between two centuries, Queen Anne's has the strength of continuity and the pioneering spirit of its founders.

Mrs. D. Forbes
September 1993

Order of Service for Opening

OPENING
OF
Queen Anne's School,
Caversham
BY THE
RIGHT REV. THE LORD BISHOP OF OXFORD,
16th May, 1894.

In the Name of the Father, and of the Son, and of the Holy Ghost.   Amen.

The Lord's Prayer

V   Our help is in the Name of the Lord,
R   Who hath made heaven and earth.
V   O God, make speed to save us.
R   O Lord, make haste to help us.
V   Glory be to the Father, and to the Son, and to the Holy Ghost.
R   As it was in the beginning, is now, and ever shall be, world without end. Amen.

Psalm VIII. *Domine, Dominus noster.*

V   The Lord be with thee.
R   And with thy spirit.

Let us pray.
Lord, have mercy upon us,
    Christ, have mercy upon us,
Lord, have mercy upon us.

V Teach me, O Lord, the way of Thy statutes.
R And I shall keep it unto the end.
V Give me understanding and I shall keep Thy law.
R Yea, I shall keep it with my whole heart.
V Lord, hear our prayer.
R And let our cry come unto Thee.

Let us pray.

ALMIGHTY and merciful God, graciously bow down Thine ear to the petitions of Thy humble servants. Grant, we beseech Thee, Thy continued blessing to this Institution for the instruction of Thy children, and vouchsafe the gift of Thy grace to all who come to learn within it, that they may grow up in Thy faith and fear, and obtain remission of all their sins, through Jesus Christ our Lord. *Amen.*

GRANT, we beseech Thee, O Lord, that a special blessing may rest upon the Governours [*sic*] and Teachers of this School, that all alike may have the help and favour of Thy grace preventing and following them, for the promotion of their work and the increase of Thy glory, through Jesus Christ our Lord.   *Amen.*

O GOD the Holy Ghost, pour down, we beseech Thee, Thy mercy upon this place, that it may be blest and hallowed by Thy presence, and that the fulness of Thy seven fold gifts may rest upon all Thy children, through Jesus Christ our Lord.   *Amen.*

O LORD God Almighty, maker of all things, and giver of all good gifts, who didst put it into the hearts of Thy servants in old days to lay the foundation of this Institution to Thy glory and praise, for the sustenance and furtherance of the Christian faith, for the benefit of Thy holy Church, and the increase of godliness among Thy people. We thank Thee for the abundant blessing which Thou has vouchsafed to the work thus begun, and for Thy watchful protection of it during near two hundred years. We thank Thee for that Thou hast permitted that, in the midst of many and great changes, it should be preserved for the holy purpose for which it was founded, and should have found a new home in a fair place. We beseech Thee, O Heavenly Father, to continue the same blessing to our children's children for all generations yet to come, that Thy faith, fear, and love may ever dwell within these walls, and ever be the safeguard of Thy daughters who shall go forth from this place to serve Thee as Thou shalt think fit to call them, until our Lord shall come again to visit us, to Whom, with Thee and the Holy Ghost, be all honour, praise, and thanksgiving, now and for evermore. *Amen.*

THE BLESSING

Appendix B

'Earliest Memories'

On that memorable May 16th 1894, my stepsister and I started from Bexhill at 6 a.m. Being a bad traveller, I was put to bed on arrival, so missed the Opening, but came down to tea on the lawn. Games followed, with Miss Holmes and her sister Rebecca looking on.

That first night I slept in the Lower Nursery in a bed by the window. Dorothy Dover, our monitress, had a large cubicle between the two doors and I was scared next morning at the clanging of the bell. Prayers and meals at first were in the dining room on the right of the entrance hall, with the wall painting of the Annunciation in the alcove opposite the window; I always admired the pot of lilies in the picture.

Beside Dorothy Dover, our other prefects were Katherine Furse, Geraldine Glencross and Hilda Euan-Smith.

We often had tea on the lawn, and ran where we liked, and climbed any trees we could; the best were a small chestnut just inside the field, and a lime-tree by the pavilion. The long rose-walk was a lovely sight in summer.

The First and Second forms started together in the end classroom near the dormitory stairs; our form mistress was Miss Emmie Mason, less strict than her sister, Esther, but both were kind and patient. We inherited the plank desks and forms used before us by the boys of Amersham Hall, with names cut deep in the wood and blackened with ink. Names and initials we found too, when we climbed up the rose ladder in the old gym, cut in the rafters. It was a tarred timber building in the Quad, near the old music cottage; it was soon pulled down, but while it lasted it was an eerie place, especially when, on a summer day, the sun shone brightly; the thick layer of tan on the floor, muffling all sound, was a warm brown, but the surrounding darkness was velvety and almost tangible.

The old music cottage had its ghost, or so we believed, on quite insufficient evidence of course. Occasionally, in the evening, the gas lights would go blue and sink; knowing nothing of pressures, we concluded it was due to a ghost, and came away as soon as possible.

The copse behind the swimming-bath was rather dark, and not a favourite haunt. We were fond of round games, especially Twos and Threes. The first attempt at uniform that I remember were the red stockings, introduced for games to ensure that we changed our black ones in coming in from the playing-field. There were loosely woven, and lost their shape very soon; it was a fearful nuisance at the Saturday afternoon mending class, in the dining hall, when we fetched our laundry and did our repairs.

One very useful institution was the Pattern Book, which we had to make, or rather to fill; a brown paper booklet into which went neat specimens of hemming, sewing, feather and other stitching, and patching, all executed in red and blue thread on white linen. I look back on these booklets now with far more appreciation than I felt while toiling at mine.

Saturday afternoon also brought 'sweets' when a table in the dining hall was laid out, and we spent our weekly pence, three in my case.

As to relations with the staff, it should be remembered that this was the Age of Respect, when authority was readily accepted, especially if there had been discipline in the home.

...

Once we went to a concert in Reading to hear Paderewski, but I regret that my chief memory is that, when the doorman announced the departures afterwards, there were a number of surprised faces in the crowd, on hearing him shout 'Queen Anne's Carriage'.

Before the chapel was built we went down to Caversham to church, and part of the way was between fields. We saw floods of 1894 from the dormitory windows.

The little Sanatorium across the road adjoined the gardens, and the green-house gave me my first sight of stephanotis and tuberose, which really did fill me 'with wonder and delight'. When Jack Hayne and I had measles in the San, and were getting better, the little old woman who looked after us wanted to go into Reading. 'Now Miss Jack and Miss Alice, promise me you won't stir from these sheets.' And we didn't, but laid them on the floor and practised war dances till we were tired.

Food was very plain; we acquired skill in carrying four or even five plates of porridge from hatches to tables. On one occasion there was a potato shortage and we had rice instead, which I still think an improvement.

...

On Ascension Day we went by pair-horse brakes to places like Nettlebed Common for a picnic. One day some Royalty was having a procession through Reading, and we had a window on the first floor at Heelas's. But for us the high-light of the afternoon was, not the Royalty, but an incident in a turning opposite. A brewer's empty dray had been stopped from turning into the main road, and about thirty people had climbed on it to see the show. Something startled the horses; they lurched, and everyone on the dray fell flat. This was fascinating; luckily no one seemed to be hurt.

...

Our clothes were plain, but most of us wore white pinafores with frills of broderie anglaise at neck and armholes, but now and then a vision would appear. The first accordion pleats were worn by Mazzie (Masarina Macready) Chute; a lovely thing with hundreds of pleats of blue nuns veiling floating from a yoke. But even more I admired a frock that Blanche Liddell wore when she and I played a duet for two pianos. It was made of crimson plush, and had very full sleeves with deep frills at the wrists, and these frills were lined with blue silk. I thought it marvellous.

...

As for Miss Holmes herself, she had remarkably blue eyes and a beautiful voice, which I seldom heard raised, and though she was not tall, she managed to give an impression of dignity. The scent of freesia always brings back moments of standing miserably in front of her table, with that voice saying 'Now tell me. WHY did you do it?'

Alice Alment (Slythe)

Appendix C

Chairmen of Governors

The Grey Coat Hospital Foundation 1879-1948

George Andrew Spottiswoode Esq	February 1879 - February 1884
John Charles Thynne Esq	26 January 1893 - 8 February 1895
Major-General Charles Alexander Sim MSBL	8 February 1895 - 30 September 1897 (death reported)
The Revd Prebendary The Hon J. S. Northcote MA	30 September 1897 - 24 March 1920
The Rt Revd Herbert E. Ryle DD CVO Dean of Westminster	24 March 1920 - 22 October 1925 (death reported)
The Revd Canon H. L. C. de Candole (acting Chairman then Chairman)	22 October 1925 - 17 December 1925
S. P. B. Bucknill Esq JP	25 March 1926 - 9 February 1928
The Revd Canon C. S. Woodward MA MC	9 February 1928 - 18 May 1933
Percy Gates Esq (acting Chairman)	18 May 1933 - 26 October 1933
The Revd Canon F. R. Barry MA DSO	26 October 1933 - 15 October 1941
The Rt Revd P. F. D. de Labillière DD Dean of Westminster	4 February 1942 - 24 January 1945
W. Wickham Legg Esq MA (acting Chairman)	24 January 1945 - 16 May 1945
The Revd Canon Adam Fox MA	16 May 1945 - 15 December 1948

From 1949 the Foundation was called 'The Royal Foundation of Grey Coat Hospital'.

The Rt Revd C. E. Curzon DD	30 March 1949 - 24 August 1954 (death reported)
Ven Archdeacon A. J. Morcom MA	17 November 1954 - 7 July 1966
Alderman Sir Harold Gillett Bt MC FCA	7 July 1966 - 28 November 1968
Ven Archdeacon J. R. G. Eastaugh BA	28 November 1968 - 9 January 1974
Ven Archdeacon S. M. F. Woodhouse MA	9 January 1974 - 12 March 1981
R. H. Clutton Esq FRICS	12 March 1981 - to date

Queen Anne's School from 1894 to date

The Chairman of the Grey Coat Hospital Foundation was Chairman of all Committees from 1894-March 1912. From that date Queen Anne's School Committee had a separate Chairman. From 1978 the Governors were members of Queen Anne's School Council.

John Charles Thynne Esq	January 1893 - February 1895
Major-General Charles Alexander Sim MSBL	February 1895 - September 1897 (death reported)
The Revd Prebendary The Hon J. S. Northcote MA	September 1897 - March 1912

(Note: Northcote continued as 'Foundation Chairman' until March 1920)

The Revd Canon G. C. Bell MA	March 1912 - January 1913
W. A. Bailward Esq	January 1913 - January 1918
No Chairman appointed for a year	
The Revd Prebendary The Hon J. S. Northcote MA	January 1919 - January 1920
Miss G. M. Ireland Blackburne STh	March 1920 - January 1929
Miss Edith Sankey JP	January 1929 - February 1955
Mrs R. E. Blair MA	February 1955 - July 1956
Lady Sykes	July 1956 - July 1963
Mrs R. E. Blair MA	July 1963 - October 1971
Dr D. Muriel Hall PhD DSc	October 1971 - 31 August 1992
Mrs P. I. Morgan JP	1 September 1992 - to date

Chairmen of the Old Girls' Society

Up to 1969	The Headmistress
1969-74	Jennifer Bowen (1943-50)
1974-78	Glenda Trench (née Lachlan, 1934-40)
1978-83	Hilary Hall (née Gamlen, 1947-53)
1983-88	Jennifer Beattie (1959-65)
1988-94	Lin Hutchinson (née Johnson, 1957-65)

Appendix D

The Prospectus

The following extract is taken from the 1917 Prospectus:

The object of the School is to afford a thoroughly good and practical education combined with moral and religious training, including instruction in the doctrines and discipline of the Church of England. The usual Services are conducted in the School Chapel. The Scheme contains a Conscience Clause applicable to day girls.

There are also four Boarding Houses sanctioned by the Governors:-

Miss E. Mason, Hillside, Henley Road, Caversham.   Terms on application.
Miss O. Lloyd, The Hill, Caversham   ditto.
Mrs. Holmes, Oakfield, Derby Road, Caversham.   ditto.
Mrs. Robinson, Parkhurst, Grosvenor Road, Caversham.   ditto.

Admission.   Girls are admitted at the age of 10 and (as a rule) up to 15, and must leave the School at the end of the School year in which the age of 18 is attained unless (in special cases) permitted by the Governors to remain a year more, on the recommendation of the Head Mistress. Girls are liable to removal at any time if they do not satisfy the Head Mistress as to progress and conduct.

Before the admission of any girl in to the School, a certificate of her good conduct and character may be required; and also a certificate as to bodily health, including satisfactory vaccination and re-vaccination.

No girl shall enter or return to School from any house in which there has been any infectious disease within the three preceding weeks, without bringing a medical certificate, and obtaining the permission of the Head Mistress. In case of any violation of this rule, the girl will immediately be sent home, and the sum paid for the term forfeited to the School.

A certificate of non-contact with infection during holidays or other absence, signed by the parent or guardian, must be sent on return to School.

The School year begins in September, and is divided into three terms; and the Spring, Summer and Christmas vacation extend to thirteen weeks or thereabouts.

All girls seeking admission will enter in order of their registration (priority being given to Westminster candidates), and will be required to pass an Entrance Examination, which is graduated according to age, and is not competitive:-

Under 12.—Reading, Writing, Arithmetic (including Vulgar and Decimal Fractions), Money Rules, easy questions in English Grammar, English History and Geography.

Over 12.—More difficult questions on above subjects, with some knowledge of Unitary Method, and an elementary knowledge of French.

Over 14.—A higher Standard in all subjects.

Appendix E

The Flu Poem

A DOGGEREL RHYME OF Q.A.S.   Autumn Term. 1918.

1. Sing a song of Flu-Time
   "Cases" coming fast.
   "New Wing", "Rooms" and "Nurseries",
   All were filled at last.
   Staff were very busy,
   Forms grew daily less,
   Wasn't that a half-term
   To spend at Q.A.S ?

2. Sing a song of day-time
   Endless trays of meals
   Endless queues in Sick-room
   Endless tramp of heels,
   Endless journeys to the "San"
   Endless fires to mend,
   Endless calls from telephone
   Endless wires to send.

3. Sing a song of night-time
   Patients all in beds,
   Suppers safely swallowed
   Pillows under heads.
   Of temperatures fiery
   Charts should records bear.
   But woe - the four thermometers
   Lie broken on the stair.

4. When half-term was over
   Still the fray went on,
   Lessons were abandoned
   Several staff were gone.
   Girls were drinking tonic
   Girls were acting plays,
   Girls were trundling home in trains,
   These were hectic days .

5. All at last was over,
   All the germs were dead,
   All the form-rooms full again,
   All the nurses fled.
   Everything was in its place,
   Everybody sane,
   But - may the Flu Fiend never come
   To Q.A.S. again .

Vesper

VESPER HYMN

Juliet Crawley-Boevey

Appendix G
1934 Calendar

Summer Term.

MAY

☀	...	6	13	20	27
M	...	7	14	21	28
Tu	1	8	15	22	29
W	2	9	16	23	30
Th	3	10	17	24	31
F	4	11	18	25	...
S	5	12	19	26	...

JUNE

☀	...	3	10	17	24
M	...	4	11	18	25
Tu	...	5	12	19	26
W	...	6	13	20	27
Th	...	7	14	21	28
F	1	8	15	22	29
S	2	9	16	23	30

JULY

☀	1	8	15	22	29
M	2	9	16	23	30
Tu	3	10	17	24	31
W	4	11	18	25	...
Th	5	12	19	26	...
F	6	13	20	27	...
S	7	14	21	28	...

AUGUST

☀	...	5	12	19	26
M	...	6	13	20	27
Tu	...	7	14	21	28
W	1	8	15	22	29
Th	2	9	16	23	30
F	3	10	17	24	31
S	4	11	18	25	...

WALKER

Appendix H
Specimen Bill

QUEEN ANNE'S SCHOOL,
Caversham, near Reading.

School Fees (Subject to Revision), Autumn Term, 1935.

Name.......... *Leahy E. M. M.* ....

	£	s.	d.
For Tuition, Books, Stationery, Apparatus, etc.	11	—	
For Board, Laundress and Doctor (ordinary)	15	13	4
Optional—Pianoforte £3 3/–, *Violin £3 3/*	—	3	3 0
Do. Organ £3 3/–, Cello £3 3/–	—	—	—
Do. Orchestra Class 7/6			
Do. Drawing £1 1/–			
Do. Dancing £1 1/–			
Do. Verse Speaking £1 10/– *Special Prefets*		7	6
Do. Insurance Premium	—	—	—

		s.	d.
	Needlework Materials	......	......
	Extra Washing *+ Cleaning*	13	1
	Damages	......	......
	Carrier, Parcels, Bus, etc.	......	......
	Mending and Ma*king*	......	......
Extras	Entertainments, *Ex*cursions	......	......
	Shoe Mending	......	......
for	Hairdresser	3	3
	Medical Comforts	9	—
Past	Sheet Music	—	—
	Handicrafts	......	......
Term.	House Tie	......	......
	Drawing Materials	......	......
	~~Remedials~~ *Birthday cake*	7	6
	Extra Fruit	5	—
	Chair in Hall	15	—

TOTAL EXTRAS **2 - 8 - 7**

£32 - 12 - 5

W. Graham Everitt

Clerk and Receiver.

N.B.—Parents and Guardians are required to give the Head Mistress a term's notice of their intention to remove a Girl from the School to take effect at end of term, or to pay a term's fee in lieu of notice.

Any Change of Address should be notified.

Appendix I
Rationing Letter

Telephone :
Reading 71582

QUEEN ANNE'S SCHOOL,
CAVERSHAM,
READING.

December 1939.

National Registration and Rationing

Your daughter's Identity Card and Ration Book are enclosed herewith.

1. National Registration & Change of Address

The Registrar General requires that changes of address should be notified within seven days of removal.

For the holiday period it is therefore necessary for you to inform your local Registration Officer that your daughter will be living with you and not at Caversham.

2. Rationing

As rationing begins on January 8th, it will be necessary for you to obtain a temporary ration card for your daughter from that date until January 16th.

To do this you should take her ordinary Ration Book to your local Food Controller as soon as possible - inform him that normally rations are obtained through School which is scheduled as a catering establishment - and request him to issue the necessary Temporary Ration card.

Please do not register your supplier's name in the ordinary Ration Book and please return both the Ration Book and the Identity Card at the beginning of next term.

(Signed)   J.ELLIOT

Appendix J

Old Girls' Dinner

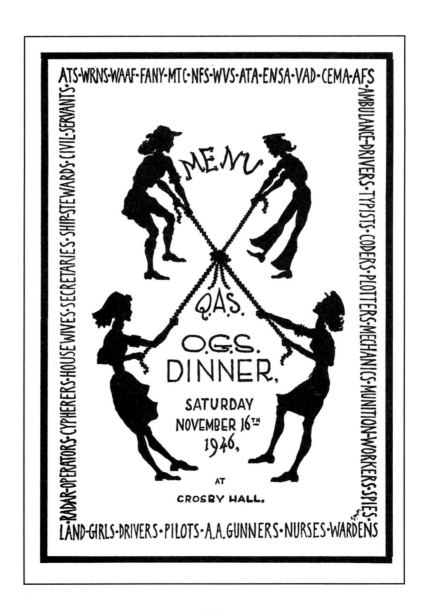

Webbe Work Sheet

Index

Former pupils and staff are indexed under maiden names. Bold page numbers refer to plates.